DORSET COUNTY LIBRARY
100528322 N

A YOUNG MAN'S WAR

The Diary and Letters
of
W. L. Ward 1918

A YOUNG MAN'S WAR

The Diary and Letters
of
W. L. Ward 1918

Alec Ward

ELLESMERE
THE MEDLAR PRESS
2008

DORSET COUNTY
11 NOV 2017
LIBRARY HQ

Published by The Medlar Press Limited,
The Grange, Ellesmere, Shropshire SY12 9DE
www.medlarpress.com

ISBN 978-1-899600-84-7

Text © Alec Ward, 2008
Design © The Medlar Press, 2008

All rights reserved. Without limiting the rights under copyright reserved above, no part of this publication may be reproduced, stored in or introduced into a retrieval system, or transmitted, in any form, or by any means (electronic, mechanical, photocopying, recording or otherwise) without the prior written permission of the Medlar Press Limited.

The Author and Publisher would like to thank Greenhill Books, London for their kind permission to reproduce an extract from Sidney Rogerson's *Last of the Ebb*, 2007.

Cover photograph:
William Leslie Ward in 1917 whilst an acting and unpaid Corporal.
His substantive rank remained Private and is shown as this on official records.

Designed and typeset in 11 on 12 point Bembo Roman
Produced in England by the Medlar Press Limited, Ellesmere, England.

Contents

Preface

My father, William Leslie Ward, joined the army in 1917. He was just eighteen. The following year he was sent to France. The big Spring 1918 German offensive was in progress. As he said later, his active service was 'brief and inglorious'. He arrived at Boulogne on 13th April. Before long he was involved as a Lewis gunner in a counter-attack at Kemmel in which his unit suffered several casualties and they took some fifty prisoners. After a rest period well behind the lines his unit took part in the battle of the Aisne and it was there, near the town of Concevreux, that on 27th May he was put out of action by a bullet wound in the leg: a 'Blighty' one. On the sketch map of the Aisne on page 8 the red dot marks the spot where he was wounded. He was hospitalised for a few weeks in France and then brought back to England. By the time he had recovered the war was over.

My father died in 1974. In clearing the house, a tin trunk full of memorabilia, mainly family photographs was discovered. The contents were put into large cardboard boxes which we took out occasionally to look at the pictures. But it was only last year (2007) that I realised the significance of the old brown envelope under the photo albums (labelled in my father's handwriting 'Letters from France 1918'). Inside, written mainly in pencil on an assortment of faded, folded pieces of paper, in places barely decipherable, were the original diary and letters written by my father while serving in France in 1918. I was quite excited by the discovery. I knew that my father had later on included in his memoirs passages about his experiences in France but I had no idea that the original source material had been preserved. Here was a piece of living history. So I spent several happy hours transcribing the documents which form the basis of this book.

Alec Ward, September 2008

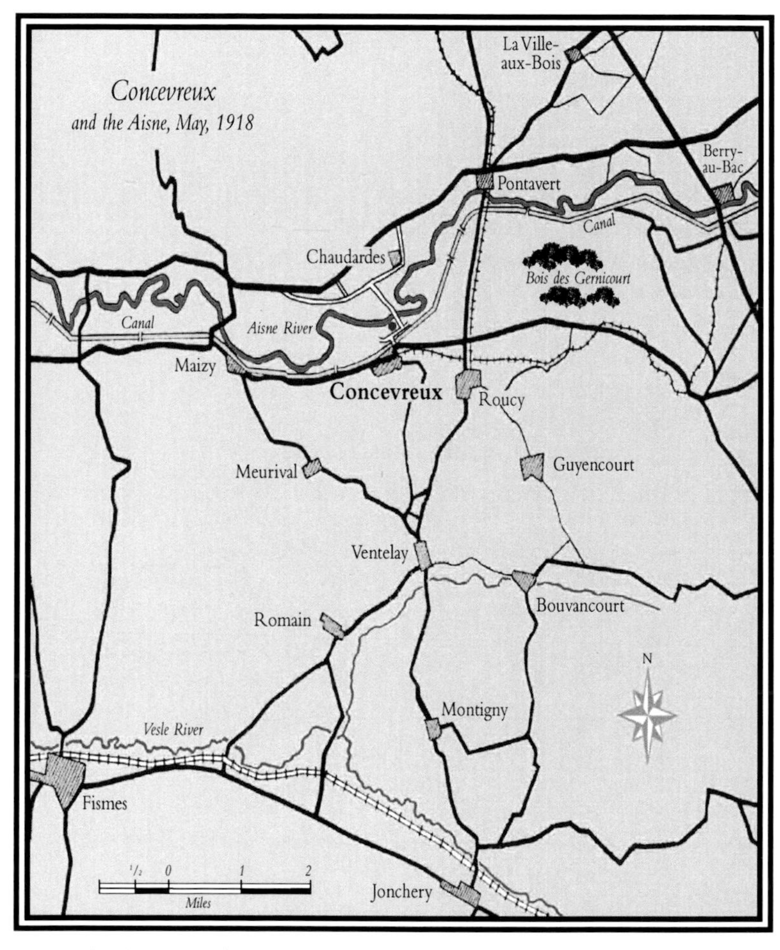

The red dot shows the field where W. L. Ward was wounded during the afternoon of 27th May, 1918.

The Silver War Badge (sometimes called the Silver Wound Badge) shown opposite and throughout the book was awarded to all who served at home or abroad after 4th August 1914, and who, on account of age, or physical infirmity arising from wounds or sickness, were unable to continue with military service. The Silver War Badge is not a medal or decoration. Each badge issued had a number engraved on the back which identified the individual.

A Young Man's War

On the afternoon of May 27th I was wounded at a point between Concevreux and its bridge over the Aisne. Two Northumberland Fusiliers retiring down the road nearby came to my help and they supported me - later almost carrying me - until we met a motor ambulance going forward. Coming under machine gun fire the driver quickly reversed and took his load to an Advanced Dressing Station. There without attention we were quickly loaded into lorries and driven off south.

My lorry had a French driver who, after encountering a little shellfire, drove over the rough roads at a rattling speed - encouraged no doubt in French taxi style, by the curses, groans and shouts of "Lentement, monsieur!" from his cargo. We arrived at a French Casualty Clearing Station near the Marne at dusk and in the early hours of the 28th I was despatched in a horsebox by rail to Paris. After a week there I went via Rouen and Le Havre to Blighty.

W. L. W.

CHAPTER 1

The First World War

ON 28TH JUNE, 1914, Archduke Ferdinand, the nephew of the ageing Habsburg Emperor of Austria-Hungary, and his heir, was assassinated in Sarajevo, the capital of Bosnia, a country annexed by Austria in 1908. Europe was shaken. A Serbian terrorist had been responsible and the Austrians thought the Serbian Government were implicated. Austria, with German backing, declared war on Serbia. Russia started mobilising her armies in support of Serbia. Germany at once declared war on Russia and, a day later, on Russia's ally France as well.

Britain had for many years avoided involvement in European conflicts ('splendid isolation') and many people thought we should not get involved in this one. German policy was to deal quickly with France and then turn and deal with Russia. But their military plan for dealing with France involved sending their armies through Belgium. Belgian independence had been guaranteed by all the European powers (Treaty of 1839) and it was the attack on Belgium on 4th August that swayed the doubters in Britain and drove the British Government to declare war on Germany that night.

Thus began the Great War or, as it came to be called later, the First World War. People thought it would all be over in months, or even weeks, as other European conflicts had been over the hundred years since Waterloo. Little did they realise what a monster was being unleashed: four years of terrible slaughter, total war involving much of the world, millions of men killed and maimed, untold civilian suffering, national economies destroyed.

In the early summer of 1914 no one in England had been expecting or wanting war. On the surface all was set fair but there were serious underlying tensions. Germany had been building up her military strength for several years and Britain, relying on naval pre-eminence to protect her worldwide trade and empire, was particularly concerned about the German naval building programme. Diplomatically Europe was divided into two camps: the Triple Alliance of Germany, Austria and Italy; and the French/Russian alliance, with Britain having understandings with France (Entente).

The British Expeditionary Force, consisting of most of her regular army, was deployed rapidly across the Channel and helped the French army check the progress of the German invaders. At least they stopped them getting to Paris or taking the Channel ports. But a stalemate was soon reached and both sides dug themselves in. So, from the winter of 1914, they faced each other from a complex of trenches stretching in a swathe from the Channel to the Swiss border. Over the next four years the broad outline of the battle fronts remained much the same. Some areas were fought over again and again. Until 1918 it was usually the allied forces who were taking the initiative, trying to drive the Germans back from occupied French and Belgian territory. But the advantages lay with the defenders. Infantry men 'going over the top' and advancing on foot across no-man's land were terribly vulnerable to German machine-gun fire. On the first day of the battle of the Somme, 1st July, 1916, the British had 60,000 casualties, including 21,000 killed. The overall ratio of allied to German casualties was about 3 to 2.

Turkey had joined Germany at the end of 1914. Faced with stalemate on the western front, the allies attempted in 1915 to send a naval force through the Dardanelles, the waterway linking the Mediterranean with the Black Sea, with the object of capturing Constantinople and opening up a supply route to their Russian allies. But the attempt failed and troops that had been landed at Gallipoli, including a large contingent of Australians and New Zealanders, had to be withdrawn after heavy losses. Other campaigns against the Turks were ultimately more successful. By the end of the war they had been driven from Mesopotamia (Iraq), Arabia, Jordan, Palestine and Syria. Many Indian troops took part in the campaigns. T. E. Lawrence helped mobilise Arabian support. The Ottoman Empire ceased to exist.

After some early losses, British naval control of the high seas was rarely disputed. Thousands of troops were brought in convoy safely from Australia and New Zealand. A tight blockade was kept on German ports. Troops and supplies for our forces in France and Belgium were maintained without interruption. A big naval battle off Jutland in 1916 was a mixed affair but at least the German fleet never put to sea again. The big problem for us was the damage done to our merchant shipping by German submarines (U-boats). In early 1917 there was a serious threat of food shortages. But the introduction of a convoy system and the use of depth charges and mines greatly reduced shipping losses.

A big blow for the allies in 1917 was the Russian revolution and their withdrawal from the war. They signed the peace treaty of Brest Litovsk with Germany in 1918. It meant that large numbers of German troops could be transferred from their eastern front to join the forces in the west. On the other hand the allies received a huge, probably decisive, boost from America's entry into the war; a decision provoked by the Germans extending submarine attacks to neutral shipping. Thousands of young Americans enlisted and started training, ready to cross the Atlantic and join the struggle.

In 1918 the Germans made one final attempt to win the war by launching a major offensive on the western front. They needed to force a decision before American troops arrived and upset the balance. They made some progress, notably in the Battle of the Aisne, the battle in which my father, W. L. Ward, was shot, but their advance ran out of steam. By early summer, fresh American troops, eager to take part, had started arriving. By September several hundred thousands had joined the battle-hardened but weary French and British troops in pushing the Germans back. There followed a collapse of German military and civilian morale (aided by American help in tightening the blockade of German ports). The allies had been expecting the war to go on into 1919 but in October the Germans gave in and sued for peace. On 9th November a Republic was proclaimed in Berlin and the Kaiser left for exile in Holland. An armistice was signed on 11th November. By then the Austrians had also given up.

So ended the war that many called 'the war that would end all wars'. Little did they think that just over twenty years later there would be another . . .

Trench Warfare

Much has been written about the horrors of trench warfare: the cramped 'dug-outs' for rest and sleeping; the 'stand to' at dawn; the tot of rum for Dutch courage before going 'over the top'; the barbed wire and the bullets; the gas, ranging from lethal to merely irritant, used by both sides; the firing squad for some 300 deserters or those who just couldn't face it; the shell-shock; the suicides and self-inflicted wounds; the hopes for a 'Blighty' one, a minor injury that would get you back to England; the awful mud; the desolate landscape of 'no-man's land' filled with shell holes and blasted trees; the stench of decomposing corpses; the terrible casualty rate; the weeks of boredom between spells of frantic life-threatening activity.

Men stayed in the front line, the 'suicide ditch', for a few days before going back to support or reserve trenches and periodically further back to rest and recreation areas where they could bathe, change their lice-ridden clothes and generally relax, play football, spend their 5-franc notes in local cafes. After a few months, there would be 'leave' in England. Junior officers took their turn in the front line. Their casualty rate was much higher than the rest: they led from the front and their uniforms - including leather Sam Browne belts, made them conspicuous targets for snipers. Senior officers were often billeted further back in requisitioned houses, paying occasional visits to their men at the front.

Food and other supplies were usually taken to the forward lines via communication trenches at night. Hot meals often arrived cold. The diet may have been boring but seems to have been adequate. Corned beef (bully) was a staple but horsemeat not unknown. Germans capturing British trenches in 1918 were astonished to find how well British troops were provided for. Supply lines back to England were a remarkable feat of organisation. Front line soldiers could look forward to daily deliveries of letters from home only three or four days old; and parcels too, often shared with comrades. Troops were encouraged to write letters home, which were meant to be censored by junior officers but not always were. Men often asked for writing materials to be sent as paper was scarce in the trenches. By 1918 the Army Postal Service employed 4000.

Canadians holding the line at Passchendaele. Photograph courtesy of Library and Archives Canada.

Comradeship flourished. Men went to great lengths to rescue the wounded, often getting hurt themselves. Wounded were treated at a range of facilities, from battlefield dressing stations to English hospitals. Many when recovered were sent back to the front again. A sense of humour and lots of songs helped to keep spirits up – 'Pack up your troubles', 'Mademoiselle from Armentieres', 'Take me back to dear old Blighty', 'It's a long way to Tipperary' and many others.

Thousands of horses and mules were used for transport and hauling guns behind the lines. By 1918 the British army was using 500,000 horses and 230,000 mules. But cavalry were of little use in trench warfare. Their place in offensive operations was eventually taken by the tank. All 474 tanks of the British Tank Corps were used to considerable effect at the battle of Cambrai in 1917. Early models often broke down or got 'ditched' in the trenches. But by the summer of 1918 British and French tanks had made trench warfare redundant and restored movement to the battlefield.

The War at Home

Anti-German feeling was fed by rumours of atrocities in Belgium, civilian air-raid casualties and the sinking of the *Lusitania* and unarmed merchant ships. German nationals were interned and anyone with a German name was suspected of hostile actions or sympathies and liable to be attacked. (Dachshund dogs had stones thrown at them!) The First Sea Lord, Prince Louis of Battenberg, a cousin of King George V, had to step down and the Battenbergs changed their name to Mountbatten. (Prince Louis was father of Earl Mountbatten of Burma and grandfather of Prince Philip, Duke of Edinburgh). George V, conscious that his German connections might be held against him, changed the Royal Family name from Saxe-Coburg-Gotha to Windsor. Kaiser Wilhelm, another cousin, was said to have let it be known that he would enjoy attending a performance of 'The Merry Wives of Saxe-Coburg-Gotha'!

Although there had been some army reforms after the Boer war, Britain, compared with Germany, was largely unprepared for war. We only had a small regular army and little modern equipment. We lagged behind particularly in artillery and machine guns. Nevertheless, my father, writing fifty years later, said it was hard to recall the enthusiasm and idealism with which Britain, particularly the young men, entered the war. Many more men than Kitchener had called for flocked to the colours during the first few months and the organisation required to train and equip them simply did not exist. The new recruits paraded for months in civilian clothes or cheap blue serge. The regular army soon crossed the Channel and many of the instructors left behind were veterans of the Boer and earlier conflicts whose knowledge of war was massively out of date. My father, aged fifteen, a soldier's son, said he was at first tremendously thrilled. Nightly he tramped to Oxford Town Hall to read the war bulletins. But he could not forget the shock of reading that our casualties at Mons in September had amounted to 2000 - enormous by Boer War standards. There was further bad news in the autumn of 1914 in the sinking of three British warships.

So it soon became clear that there was not going to be any speedy allied victory and, as the casualties mounted, that we were in for a long haul in which the whole nation would be involved. Air raids by Zeppelin airships and Gotha bombers caused 1000 or so civilian deaths, mainly in London. New government departments were set up to control every aspect of national life. A massive effort was launched to produce shells and other munitions for the British Expeditionary Force (BEF). There was full employment. Trade Unions co-operated and strikes went down. Women suffragettes stopped their protests. Women were involved as never before in munitions factories, hospitals, agriculture and as secretaries in government departments and businesses. Conscription for men under forty was introduced in January 1916 to deal with the problem of 'slackers' but was hardly needed to affect the flow of recruits. Censorship was introduced under the Defence of the Realm Act (DoRA). Food, clothing and fuel were sometimes short and there were queues at shops. Panic buying in late 1917 led to rationing being introduced in early 1918, mainly to even out distribution. No one starved. The wheat harvest in 1917 was a record. No new houses were built. The Government borrowed on a huge scale. The National Debt was fourteen times greater in 1918 than in 1914.

Volunteers joining up at Birtley, County Durham, August 1914.

★ ★ ★

The deaths in battle of so many young men brought grief and loss to countless families. For Britain the figure was some 800,000. Every town and village War Memorial bears witness to the tragedy. One town in Lancashire had lost 517. Many families lost more than one of its members. In addition there were possibly twice as many injured, with lost limbs or permanently weakened by gas attacks or nervous illness. Casualties were about three times heavier among junior officers than with 'other ranks'. This struck at the highest in the land, young men often straight out of the best schools and colleges.

In some ways peace in the short term brought fewer problems than many had feared. By mid-1919 four out of five men in the army had been demobilised. Most were reabsorbed into the economy fairly easily. Women left many of their war-time jobs. War-time controls were lifted and for a couple of years there was something of an economic boom. But from 1921 onwards things got worse. Unemployment rose above two million that year. Strikes and threats of strikes grew, particularly in the railways and the coal industry which were returned to private ownership. Promises of 'homes for heroes' proved hard to meet.

CHAPTER 2

W. L. Ward

MY FATHER was born over a stable shortly before Xmas 1898. (As he said in his memoirs, those who knew him might not see any significance in this!) His birth was at Fulford barracks in York where the horses were stabled below the married quarters. His father, William Robert Ward, was a Sergeant in the 3rd Dragoon Guards. In January that year, after a long period of service in India, he had married his cousin, Grace Amelia Shephard. Their families both came from Boston, Lincolnshire. William Robert's father was a Master Brushmaker in the town, Grace Amelia's father was a Master Mariner who became Boston Harbour and Dockmaster. Father's parents were grandchildren of William Shephard, also a Lincolnshire Mariner, and his wife Mary.

After postings in Dublin, where my father's sister Grace was born in 1900, and South Africa at the end of the Boer War, in 1904 my grandfather began a home posting as Sergeant Major with the Oxford Yeomanry. So it was in Oxford that my father spent his schooldays. In 1912 his father retired from the army and took a job with the Oxford Canal Company looking after the coal wharves and the family moved to 'Canal House' in Worcester Street. (The house was demolished in the 1930s when the canal basin was filled in to make way for Nuffield College and a car park.)

When the First World War broke out in 1914 Ward senior re-enlisted as Regimental Sergeant Major with a second Regiment of the Oxford Yeomanry. After a few weeks as a junior clerk, my father, still under sixteen, took over his job (as Wharfinger) at the Canal basin. His terrier dog, mentioned in his letters from France (the 'Rat catcher'), helped to catch rats as the last of the coal was unloaded from the barges. All told, my father recalled his two years in charge at the Canal as a pleasant interlude before going into the army.

When he was seventeen he joined the volunteer corps, the First War equivalent of the Second War Home Guard, known locally as 'The Gorgeous Wrecks' from the GR (George Rex) on their uniforms. They paraded during the week and often on Sundays did real war work such as unloading military stores at the Ordnance Depot at Didcot.

In the early part of the war there was no shortage of volunteers to join the Services in response to Kitchener's call 'Your country needs you'. But enthusiasm waned as casualties mounted and in 1916 conscription was brought in. Under a scheme named after the War Minister, Lord Derby, young men under joining up age could register their willingness to serve and could wear arm bands to protect them from being presented with white feathers by women who thought they should be in uniform. My father did so register.

In January 1917 he enlisted. He wanted to join the Royal Horse Artillery but instead was put down for the Oxford Yeomanry, his father's regiment. The family connection helped in some ways such as the quality of his uniform. Some of the sergeants used to refer to his father affectionately as 'old rubber guts'. So my father became 'young rubber'!

The next fifteen months were spent in training and guard duties in the UK. He went on an NCOs' course emerging as an Acting Lance Corporal, and a Scouting and Bombing course where he came out top in the Brigade.

In January 1918 the regiment went to Dublin where the aftermath of the Easter 1916 Rising had left a difficult security situation. It was from there he left for France in April. His father had been invalided out of the regiment with a weak heart some weeks before.

CERTIFIED COPY OF AN ENTRY OF BIRTH
(6 & 7 Wm. IV., cap. 86).

GIVEN AT T

REGISTRATION DISTRICT YORK

BIRTH in the Sub-District of Walgate in the County Borough of ... in the County

1899										
No.	When and Where Born	Name, if any	Sex	Name and Surname of Father	Name and Maiden Surname of Mother	Rank or Profession of Father	Signature, Description and Residence of Informant	When Registered	Signature of Registrar	Baptismal Name, if added after Registration of Birth
277	Twelfth December 1898 Cavalry Barracks Gate Fulford York U.D.	William Leslie	Boy	William Robert Ward	Grace Amelia Ward formerly Shepherd	Sergeant 3rd Dragoon Guards	William R. Ward Father Cavalry Barracks York	Fifth January 1899	H.M. Foster Registrar	———

CERTIFIED to be a true Copy of an Entry in the Certified Copy of a Register of Births in the Dist...
Given at the General Register Office, Somerset House, London, under the Seal of the said Office, the 2...

CAUTION.—Any person who (1) falsifies any of the particulars on this Certificate, or (2) uses a falsified cer...

B 40948

CERTIFICATE OF BAPTISM.

Solemnized in the WESLEYAN-METHODIST CHAPEL ... York
in the County of York in the year 1899

When Baptized.	Child's Name and Sex	Parents' Name: Christian.	Parents' Name: Surname.	Abode.	Child's Age when Baptized	The Minister by whom the Baptism was solemnized
1899 January 11th No. 459	William Leslie	William Robert and Grace Amelia	Ward	24 Cavalry Barracks York	Born Dec. 12th 1898	[illegible]

2nd Feb. 1899

I Certify that the above is a true copy of an entry in the Register Book for Baptisms, solemnized in the Wesleyan-Methodist Chapel ... in the County of York

Wesleyan-Methodist Minister

Left: early photo of William Robert with Grace Amelia.

Below: my father, William Leslie and his birth and baptism certificates.

Right: my father's parents, William Robert and Grace Amelia Ward.

Below: Queen's Own Oxfordshire Hussars at George V's coronation, 22nd June, 1911. Sergeant Major William Robert Ward, second row, seated third from right.

William Leslie Ward.

William Leslie with his father.

CHAPTER 3

The Diary and Letters

My father wrote his memoirs about fifty years after he returned from France. They describe his time there and provide the context for the letters he wrote - which follow.

From the Memoirs

My active service was brief and inglorious. Landing at Boulogne on April 13th, we went up to the base camp at Etaples, where everything was in a state of mild confusion following the big German offensive of March and another which had just started on the Lys front. Drafts were being sent up to depleted units as fast as they arrived and our draft was posted to the Worcestershire Regiment although we were destined for our county regiment, the Oxford and Bucks Light Infantry. Indeed the title of the latter is on my medals.

We found the remains of the 3rd Batt. Worcesters 'resting' at the village of St Marie Capelle, not far from Poperinge. On the strength of firing a short burst I was told I was a Lewis Gunner. I had never seen that weapon before. After a week or so we were ordered up and counter-attacked at Kemmel, which the French had lost a few hours before we went in at 3 a.m. We took most of the village but as the French, on our right, had not left their trenches, we had to fall back some distance when daylight came.

'Recruits first march'. (Postcard kept with letters, with handwritten inscription.)

There followed some days of trench holding in fairly heavy shellfire and in very inadequate cover.

About the end of April we were relieved and marched to a railhead and entrained in the usual horseboxes[1] for a meandering rail journey of thirty-six hours. We were finally decanted at the peaceful station of Fere-en-Tardenois in the Aisne district. Here we came under French Army orders.

The day we arrived was warm and sunny; fuchsias and other flowers abounded and we felt grateful for the change from the dull, war-torn landscape of the Ypres area with its widespread shelling.

It transpired that four battered British divisions had been sent south, partly to recuperate and absorb drafts of young soldiers and partly to take the place of French troops who had been sent north to the assistance of the British army which was taking the brunt of the year's offensives. The Aisne front was regarded as a quiet one having had little fighting since the disastrous Nivelle offensive of a year before. This had been the main cause of the mutiny in the French army and had led to Petain's defensive and conservation policy . . . Rumours, however, were already arriving for a coming German offensive on the Chemin des Dames area, but these the French command continued to discount.

'Lord French's inspection'. (Postcard kept with letters, with handwritten inscription.)

Field Marshal John French, 1st Earl of Ypres, was a British officer serving as the first Commander-in-Chief of the British Expeditionary Force (BEF) in World War I. He was replaced in December 1915 by General Sir Douglas Haig.

Three of the four British divisions were already in the line and ours in reserve. Towards the end of May we moved up to the line of the Vesle river. Then, on the afternoon of the 26th, three German deserters came, and after cross-examination said that the German offensive would start at 4 a.m. on 27th.

We marched up in the night, which was a warm one. When the German bombardment started, using a proportion of gas-shells, we marched in gas-masks.

By dawn the line of the Aisne had already been lost but we sent gun teams forwards and I must have been one of the battalion's earliest casualties.

There must have been a guardian angel watching over me that day for, before I got a machine-gun bullet through the leg, another had hit my steel helmet and cut a groove in the side. Two Northumberland Fusiliers who were retiring down a nearby road came to my help and supported between them I reached a motor ambulance. We were fired on before the vehicle could be turned round but got clear and the load of wounded was unloaded at a Field Ambulance, itself in the process of clearing out. A French lorry took us on board and set off at a break-neck pace for we were still being shelled. It was tough on some of the more badly wounded, but one of our number ultimately produced the word '*lentement*' and the pace slackened a little.

We reached a Casualty Clearing Station[2] somewhere on the Marne and from there I went, once again in a horsebox, to Paris. The Canadian hospital at St Cloud received us, the first British wounded they had taken, and my lousy clothes were removed and my boot cut away and the leg splinted.

It is impossible (although I can still go part of the way) to recreate the ecstasy of joy and relief - provided the wound was not too serious - that one experienced in translation from the fighting line to the peace, comfort and feeding of a base hospital. In the line, when the ruling of 'two hours on and two hours off' prevailed it was never possible to get more than ninety minutes of sleep at a time. Now one could doze most of the day and night. Food and drink had been tainted by dirt and petrol or chlorination and were uncertain in quantity and delivery. Now well-cooked food was brought to you on a tray while gorgeous ladies hovered round anxious to satisfy many, if not all, of one's needs. Lovely days!

German troops, at the Battle of the Aisne, 27th May, 1918.
Courtesy of the Imperial War Museum.

The bridge at Pontavert on the Aisne. Germans being ferried across.
Courtesy of the Imperial War Museum.

After a week in Paris I moved on to Rouen. Another week there and a large batch of us sailed in a hospital ship from Le Havre to Southampton.

On the quay there RAMC orderlies came round asking what our home towns were. Of course I said "Oxford" and was told, "Right, mate, No. 3 train for you." No. 3 train duly pulled up at Oxford station, but on the centre track where it stood for about ten minutes. From my stretcher I could see the roof of Canal House, my home. The train moved on, however, and chugged away for hours until we reached Warrington! The County Asylum at Winwick had become a hospital and I spent five or six weeks there, rather badly fed, while Father got busy on the 'old boys' network' to secure my transfer to Oxford. He was successful and I made the journey south on my own. I was using crutches now and, when I had to change, hopped along on these dragging my kitbag behind me. Wounded soldiers were not rarities now and nobody paid much attention to them. In fact, when I met an old acquaintance at Oxford station, he merely said, "Hurt your leg at football?"

And so I came home.

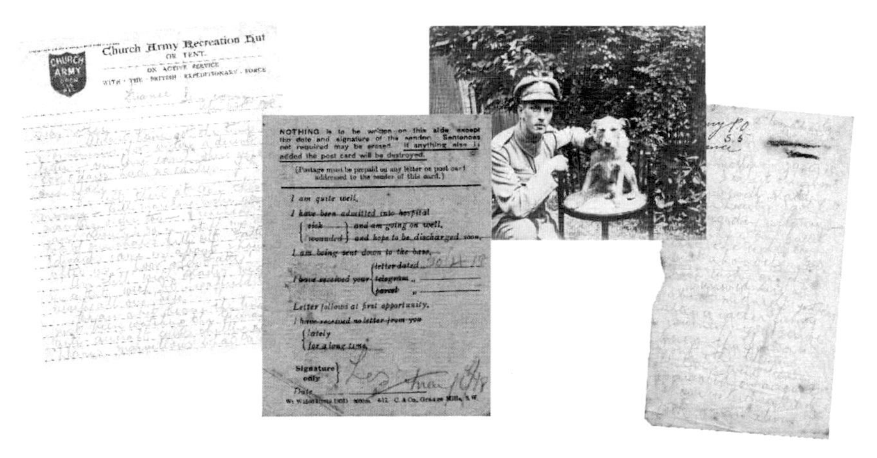

DIARY April 11th

Draft sailed from Dublin at 4 p.m. Arrived Holyhead 7.30. Immediately marched to Holyhead rest camp where we stayed in huts until 12 midnight - had one issue of terribly strong tea.

POSTCARD April 11th

Draft left D 4 p.m. Now in Holyhead rest camp. Only have few hours. Not certain whether stopping in England a bit or going straight out.

DIARY April 12th

Paraded about 12.30 a.m. and marched down to Holyhead station and entrained. Left at 2.30 a.m. Started eating rations of bully and bread. At Rugby we had our breakfast consisting of two rounds bread and butter and a mug of coffee - went down very well too. Arrived Shorncliffe station at 1 p.m., fell in and marched to rest camp which consisted of a cluster of private houses surrounded by a fencing. 5 p.m. tea - two very small pieces of bread and jam and a canteen of tea. Spent the evening in Folkestone - very last night in England and wonder for how long. Found a very good

Y.M.C.A. hut where we wrote our first letters home since leaving Ireland. I'm sure they are very anxious for news. Had a very good supper of chips, bread then tea - then a walk back to camp along the "prom" with Blades and Hinton. Got back about 9 p.m. and were soon down to sleep.

LETTER from Folkestone
Y.M.C.A. April 12th

Dear Mother,
At last have got time to write a decent letter. We are now in the rest camp here, just been for a walk on the sea front, beautiful day - quite hot.

Well this draft has been quite the biggest hustle I ever experienced. We knew nothing of the order to move until 9.30 on Thursday morning and all 3 drafts had to parade at 1.30 for moving off.

During the morning we had to draw rifles, hand in kit, get rations, pay and all the other odds and ends which Dad knows of.

The poor old Col [Colonel] was terribly upset. He only managed to say a few words and then stood there mopping his eyes - poor old Peter.

Pitt was sergeant of the guard and when we marched out tears were rolling down his face as he stood at the "present". I think he was very cut up at not being able to say goodbye to us all.

The boat sailed at 4 p.m. - the Wilts, Somersets and Worcesters came with us - nearly 900 in all. The Royal Irish band played us off at the quay.

Reached Holyhead at 8 p.m. and then marched up to Holyhead rest camp where we managed to get a few hours' sleep - paraded again at midnight and marched down to the station again where our train left at 2.15 a.m. The train went right thro to Shorncliffe station where we arrived at 12.45 p.m. Had our breakfast at Rugby - mug of coffee and bread and butter.

Our rest camp is a fine place. One block of about 20 big lodging houses, they put about 60 in each house. Blades, Hinton, Luff and I have got a room to ourselves so far.

Sgt Swaffield said that No. 3 draft will in all probability stay at the rest camp for some days as it consists mainly of A2 men.[3]

The Channel looks lovely this afternoon. A convoy of ships had just started when we were on the front and the destroyers and airships made a very pretty sight.

There is a very good Y.M.C.A. here. Just had something to eat. Food at the Rest Camp seems very good and plentiful.

Major Beaver and another O.B.L.I.[4] officer are in charge of us, very good chaps, always pushing us on first . . . *[page missing]*

DIARY April 13th

Parade at 8.30 and drew rations for the day, then marched down to the quay to embark for France. I wonder how many poor devils have trod that path since '14. Boat left about 10.30. Just behind there was another filled with a Chinese labour unit. Boulogne reached at 12.30. Very smooth passage. Formed up outside the docks. Marched off to the strains of a military band. Had dinner at the officer's rest billet: cheese, white bread, marg, tea and salmon - so far so good. Left Boulogne in the afternoon for Etaples. The French . . . [railway was too crowded to take] our chaps; half of them running alongside the train for a considerable distance, while a few preferred sitting on top. Just before we reached Etaples part of the train seemingly jumped the rails and overturned. Major Beaver (DCO)[5] got a bad shaking up but recovered enough to take charge, although walking with a limp. Etaples is a dreary looking place. We are in tents & in a very sandy spot, bitterly cold wind, drew a groundsheet and blanket and settled down for the night. Y.W. S. full up but managed to get a few bars of chocolate.

LETTER April 14th, on Y.M.C.A. paper headed 'On Active Service With the British Expeditionary Force'

Dear Mother,

Expect you've been wondering where I've got to. Well, have landed safely in France and am now in a big base camp, reminds you a bit of Wivenhoe[6] with the sand all round.

We left Folkestone at 10.30 Sat morning and landed at Boulogne at 1 a.m. then went to a rest billet where we had dinner - tea, bread and marg, cheese and salmon, then marched to station and entrained.

These French trains would make you laugh. Most of our chaps were walking alongside most of the time and several were on the roof.

Our journey ended by a carriage falling off the line, luckily it was a first class coach. Major Beaver got a bad shaking up but I think he was the only casualty.

We then marched about half a mile to this camp. There are 8 corporals in our tent, but in the others there are 20 men, nice tight fit you bet.

Horribly cold wind here. We are all sitting around the tent smoking and writing.

Don't know how long we shall stick here, but expect we shall soon be moving further up the line.

I think 155 of us are going to one regiment. Will let you know my address when we are settled down.

Well I think I will close now.

With best love to all,

Les

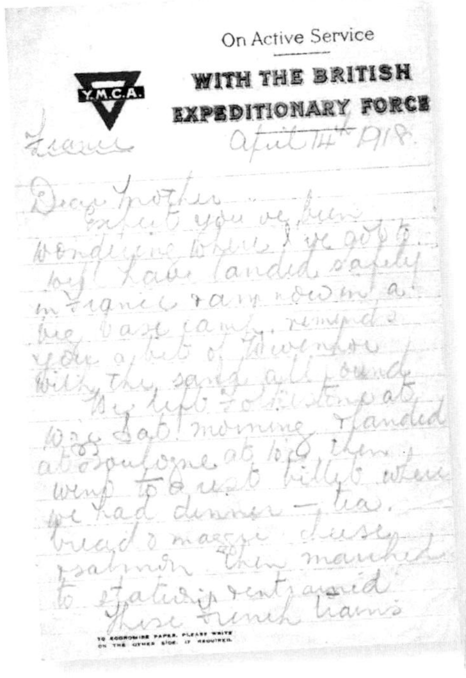

On Active Service

Y.M.C.A.

WITH THE BRITISH EXPEDITIONARY FORCE

France April 14th 1918

Dear Mother

Expect you've been wondering where I've got to. Well I have landed safely in France & am now in a big base camp, reminds you a bit of Tidworth with the sand all round. We left Folkestone at 10.30 Sat morning & landed at Boulogne at 1 p.m. then went to a rest billet where we had dinner — tea, bread & marge cheese & salmon then marched to station & entrained. These French trains

TO ECONOMISE PAPER, PLEASE WRITE ON THE OTHER SIDE IF REQUIRED.

would make you laugh. Most of our chaps were walking alongside most of the time & several were on the roof. Our journey ended by a carriage falling off the line, luckily it was a first class coach, Maj. Beaver got a bad shaking up but I think he was the only casualty. We then marched about ½ mile to this camp. there are 8 corporals in our tent, in the others there are 20 men, nice tight fit you bet. Horribly cold wind here. We are all sitting round the tent smoking & writing

LETTER April 16th
on page torn from notebook

Dear Mother,
Still knocking about behind the lines. We moved up yesterday to a place about 20 kilometres (14 miles) behind the lines. You can hear the guns here but very faintly.

We are under canvas as before but grass this time, not sand, thank goodness.

The whole of our draft, with the exception of about 20, have been transferred from the O.B.L.I. to the 3rd battalion Worcesters.

The train journey yesterday lasted from 10 a.m. to 6.30 p.m., in the usual French style about an average of 10 miles an hour.

It is impossible to give any address at present but expect shall be joining our unit soon, in that case will send it at once.

Blades and I are in the same tent with Cpl Cox, Morris, Stanley, all Oxfords.

Weather is much warmer today, but still dull.

Only good news came down today, Fritz has retired some 14 miles, of course we see no papers here. The guns are thudding away now, evidently Fritz is copping it hot.

Well, will close now as have got no real news.

Best love to all.
Excuse paper.
Les

POSTCARD 18th April
Field Service / Multiple choice

I am quite well.

Letter follows at first opportunity.

Les

A.F.A. 2042.
114/Gen. No./5248.

FIELD SERVICE
POST CARD

The address only to be written on this side. If anything else is added the post card will be destroyed.

[Crown Copyright Reserved.]

NOTHING is to be written on this side except the date and signature of the sender. Sentences not required may be erased. If anything else is added the post card will be destroyed.

[Postage must be prepaid on any letter or post card addressed to the sender of this card.]

I am quite well.

~~I have been admitted into hospital~~

~~sick~~ ~~and am going on well.~~

~~wounded~~ ~~and hope to be discharged soon.~~

~~I am being sent down to the base.~~

~~I have received your~~ ~~letter dated~~ ~~telegram~~ ,, ~~parcel~~ ,,

Letter follows at first opportunity.

~~I have received no letter from you~~ ~~lately~~ ~~for a long time.~~

Signature only

Date 18-4-17

W4 1566—R1619. 6,000,000 11.17 S. & S., Ltd. E. 1418.

LETTER headed 'France. Sun evening April 21st 1918.
Church Army Recreation Hut or Tent.
On active service with the British Expeditionary Force.'

Dear Mother,
At last we have got the time and the conveniences for writing a decent letter - our last camp where we were for 5 days had no canteen, Y.M. or such place.

We left there at 9 o.c. this morning - full marching order too - and reached this camp about 2.30 p.m. Stiff march. Lots of our chaps fell out. Fatty Edwards came in about 2 hours after us - poor old Fatty.

Am still with Blades. We are in a tent with Sgt Swaffield, Coleman, nearly all our boys.

We are a bit nearer the line now. Just been watching the German anti-aircraft guns shelling our planes. Marvellous what a lot of ammunition they waste without touching them.

We have had to bivouac for the last two nights. Blades and I soon rigged up a roof with our groundsheets and slept quite warm, although there was a frost every night.

The weather is much warmer today and I am just beginning to enjoy the life. Am feeling quite fit thank goodness.

We are moving up to join our battalion now. Shall be able to send my address soon.

There's a big gun firing just near here, makes a hell of a row. Hope he doesn't get busy tonight.

Am writing this in a Church Army hut. They've sold out of everything except writing tables and they're pretty full.

Had an issue of tobacco this morning and managed to wangle 1/4 lb of tobacco. Most of the chaps got 20 fags.

Coleman is Acting Q.M. Sergeant for our party. I expect he wishes he could keep the job, but he's not got enough push - gets done down every time.

We were paid last night ten francs (8/-) each, just getting used to French money - rather awkward at first.

I hope you have received that haversack of odds and ends of mine - I gave it to Hodges to send on the morning we came away.

Well I think I have got no more news so will close now.

With very best love to all of you.

Les

Monday 2 p.m. Just arrived at Worcesters hutments.
Address:
Pte W. L. Ward 57319
No 4 Platoon
"B" Coy[7]
3rd Battn. Worcester Regt.
B.E.F.
Just got Grace's letter dated April 18th.

PLEASE HELP US TO ECONOMIZE BY WRITING ON BOTH SIDES OF THIS PAPER.

Church Army Recreation Hut
OR TENT.
ON ACTIVE SERVICE
WITH · THE · BRITISH · EXPEDITIONARY . FORCE

France Sun. evening
April 21st 1918

Dear Mother,
At last, have got the time and convenience for writing a decent letter — our last camp where we were for 5 days had no canteen, Y.M. or such place.
We left there at 9 o/c this morning — full marching order, some marching order too — I reached this camp about 1.30 p.m. still many lots of our chaps fell out. Fatty Edwards came in about 3 hours after us — poor old Fatty!
Am still with Gladys we are in a tent with Sgt. Swaffield Coleman nearly all our boys.
We are a bit nearer the line now. just been watching the German anti-aircraft guns shelling our planes. marvellous what a lot

Field Service POSTCARD *of April 30th 1918*

I am quite well
Letter follows at first opportunity

LETTER of May 4th 1918, Church Army paper

Dear Mother,
Just received Grace's letter dated April 30th.

I am so very sorry I have not been able to get one off before now but we have been up the line for 8 days and I was only able to get a Field Postcard off on Tuesday last, just before we went into the front line for the second time.

I think our draft got a pretty good baptism of fire. We left our camp on Thurs aft., marched up the line and dug ourselves in under shell fire and were then told we were to make a counter-attack on a certain village[8] just taken by Fritz.

It began to rain about 1 a.m. and I woke up to find I was sitting in a nice little pool of it, so altogether we felt pretty cheery you can bet.

We had no trenches to take off from, just marched down a road - came under machine gun fire, deployed and carried on with the attack which began about 2.30 a.m. I should think.

Our battalion gained its objective but had to retire in the morning owing to the troops on the right having failed to advance.

We were relieved on Sat. night and were in the reserve trenches until Tues. night when we went up to the front line again and were finally relieved on Thurs. night.

Our division is now out for a good rest.

Our billet for tonight is an old barn practically out of gunfire. I think we are moving further back tomorrow.

I haven't heard for certain of the casualties in the draft, only about 6 killed I think. Powell, Winspear, Fortnum, Markwith and one or two others. Wounded: Sgt Wilkins, Cpl Cox, Bygrave, Coleman, Langford, Batts, Collett and some 20 others. None of them serious I think except Wilkins. I shouldn't be surprised if he lost a leg, got caught by a shell when advancing. Most of the wounds were machine gun bullets - nice Blighty ones.

Food is jolly good here, you needn't worry about that - rations for today were bread, marmalade, cheese, bacon, porridge, tea and stew.

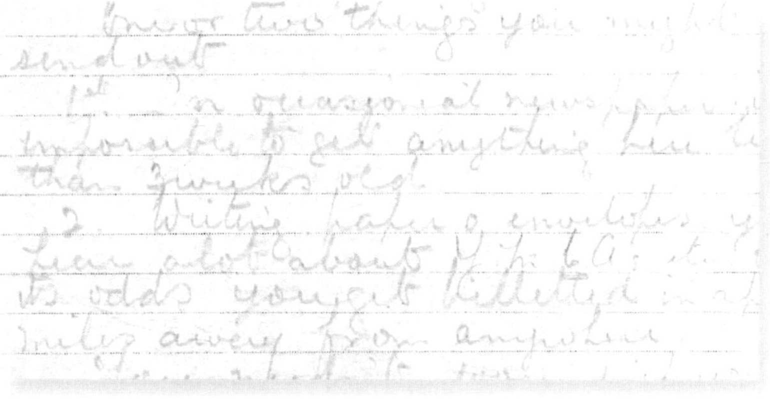

One or two things you might send out

1st. An occasional newspaper, it's impossible to get anything here less than 3 weeks old.

2. Writing paper and envelopes. You hear a lot about Y.M.C.A.s etc but its odds you get billeted on a place miles away from anywhere.

You needn't worry if you don't hear from me for a week or more at a stretch as when we are on the line it is impossible to get a letter away sometimes - depend I'll write when I can

Sorry to hear Dad isn't well - tell him to buck up and K. D.[9] as Armand[10] says.

Well I think I have about exhausted my news so will close. Don't forget to write even if you don't hear from me.

Love to all.

Les

Field Service POSTCARD *May 6th 1918*

I am quite well. Letter follows at first opportunity.

France
7. 15 18.

Dear Mother
Received your letter April 28th
yesterday – evidently been delayed
somewhere as I got Gracie's letter written
on the 30th about 3 days ago
We have been on the move ever
since we were relieved on May 2nd
& we are now just outside a nice little
town about 20 miles behind the lines.
I think we are moving still further
back tomorrow – we are either going
to a quiet front or going to have a
good rest.
We are staying at a farm, sounds
nice doesn't it. but it's the barn
that we occupy – about 800 us
Raining cats & dogs now. so all we can
do is sit on our kits & read. write &
smoke.
Blades & I went up into the town
last night had a good feed at
the Ex. Force Canteen first. then bought
some rolls. chocolate & a magazine or two
& came back to have a read in bed.
You needn't [illegible] but one thing
sending a parcel out – something to
I should like – something
thing on bread fish paste or something
of the sort you see you get about
1/3 of a loaf for bread ration & enough
jam to go on about 2 slices!

Letter of May 7th

Dear Mother,
Received your letter April 28th yesterday - evidently been delayed somewhere as I got Grace's letter written on the 30th about 3 days ago.

We have been on the move ever since we were relieved on May 2nd and we are now just outside a nice little town[11] about 20 miles behind the lines. I think we are moving still further back tomorrow - we are either going to a quiet front or going to have a good rest.

We are staying at a farm, sounds nice doesn't it. But its the barn that we occupy, about 80 of us. Raining cats and dogs now so all we can do is sit on our tails and read, write and smoke.

Blades and I went into the town last night. Had a good feed at the Ex. Force[12] canteen first, then bought some rolls, chocolate and a magazine or two and came back to have a read in bed.

You needn't be afraid of the temptations of French towns; the only thing I am tempted to do is to eat too much and am stopped in that by the extravagant price most of these French people ask for their stuff. I always go to our own canteens; you can get stuff there very cheap and good.

Yes, I had some fun last night trying to make my wishes understood when we [went] shopping, but nearly all the people in the towns have a smattering of English thro' having troops quartered with them for over 3 years.

I told you when I answered Grace's letter what things I wanted but here's an addition - a tube of <u>solid ink tablets</u> for my pen. You can get them at Colegroves I should think; they're made by the Swan people.

Had a beautiful bath at the Army baths in the town yesterday - you get one every time you come out of the line and hand in all your dirty underclothing for clean stuff.

Father is evidently cultivating quite a circle of officer acquaintances. He must be having a fine time. Has he settled on what he's going to do yet?

Sorry Uncle Jack is not doing so well. I can't understand him wanting to come out here again but of course his work was a bit different to ours. I don't mind being in the front line, it's the getting there and coming out that whacks you - full kit, 4 drums of

Lewis gun ammunition - plenty of mud and Johnny shelling like blazes and a pitch black night.

We get plenty of tobacco out here. I reckon I've drawn nearly a pound since I have been out here and have still got about 6 oz on me.

You needn't trouble about sending a parcel out, but one little thing I should like - something to go on bread, fish paste or something of the sort. You see you get about 1/3 of a loaf for bread ration and enough jam to go on about 2 slices.

So Jimmy has got his ticket. I suppose he's happy at last. I wonder how much foolscap it cost him!

Well I don't think I have got any more news so will close.

With fondest love to all.

Les

My regards to G.F.S.A. & other enquirers.

Field Service POSTCARD *of May 11th*

I am quite well. Letter follows at first opportunity.

LETTER *of May 11th*

Dear Mother,

Just got your letter of May 6th. Surprised you haven't heard from me since we went into action. I sent a Field Card on April 30th which should have arrived within 4 days. Still you'll have got some of my letters written during the past week by now I hope.

We continued our move on Wednesday night when we left Wormhoudt and marched about 12 miles to the railway station where we entrained about 2 a.m. Thurs evening.

We were travelling for 36 hours, about the longest journey I've done, there were 43 of us in our truck and we were just about tired of each other's faces when we arrived at our destination[13] at dinner time yesterday.

Our division has been sent down here for a rest. We are right out of the British front amongst the French.

The weather is jolly hot here - am beginning to assume my

summer tint - nice, rich brown!

Blades and I went for a walk in the village last night but there was nothing to be had but figs - of all things! I hope they soon start a YMCA or canteen here.

Very quiet front here, sort of place where they only have a gun every 10 mins, not like the last place where you get about 10 a sec.

Glad to hear Dad's clock[14] has arrived, quite a Big Ben by your letter!

You say you have written me 10 letters, then I must have quite a little budget due for I've only had 4 or 5 since I landed.

Had another letter from Armand the other day. Said he had been to Oxford for a day or two.

We are living in French huts - good places - beds are built bunk fashion, one row on top of the other.

Just heard that Sgt Wilkins is dead,[15] you may have heard, if so let me know; I could see he had got it pretty bad - I was only a few yards from him when he was hit.

Very pretty country round here - very open with no hedges to be seen - there are a lot of Italian labour troops near here - first I've seen in France.

Well I think I'll knock off now.

Best love to all.
Les

LETTER *of May 13th*

Just recd Grace's letter of May 9th. I got yours of the 7th yesterday so letters are bucking up a bit.

Very sorry to hear that poor Uncle has gone. I little thought when I last saw him that he wouldn't recover - please send Auntie my very deepest sympathy with her in her loss.

The weather here seems very changeable - for the first two days it was quite hot, yesterday (Sunday) it rained all day, while it has been quite cold today and has just started to rain again this evening.

I went to church yesterday morning. The Wesleyan service of the Brigade was held in a French canteen in the village - chaplain is quite a young fellow.

I expect by now you are beginning to get my letters, written since we came out of the line (May 2nd). When you are in the line you can only send field cards and green envelopes[16] (the latter when you can get them!)

Things seem very quiet down on this front, it'll be quite a rest cure I expect for some of the old hands who have been hard at it since the push started.

So Dad has got another 5/- pension, he'll be getting quite a millionaire soon!

I went sick with my teeth this morning, the doctor said he would send me down to a dental hospital as soon as he could - I expect that would mean some time down there - all counts to the end of the war you know!

So Grace is keeping my old racket in trim, doesn't she find it a bit heavy - 14 ozs is supposed to be a man's weight!

Yes, I heard that Barnes was a prisoner when I was last home on leave, didn't know that Major Taylor was tho'.

The company has been hard at it all day drilling. I'm on a machine gun course at present - nice soft job as Dad will tell you. I was on the gun team when we were up the line - the only thing I don't like is lugging the magazine about wherever you go! You know I never did like work.

I expect letters take about 5 days from here - I always write in the evening and they aren't collected until the following day and then they have a pretty good way to go to the base from our front; your's posted on May 10th is the quickest I've had, only took 3 days.

Coleman will soon be out again. I should think he only got a flesh wound in the arm. If I catch one I shall want a real "Blighty", say 3 or 4 months would just about suit me!

You'd be surprised how pleased some chaps are when they get hit. I remember a chap who was out with me on patrol one day was wounded in the leg and foot and while we were tying him up he seemed as pleased as punch about it!

Blades and I are still together with a lot of other boys, Firley, Bray, Coates etc in our platoon.

Well I think I've about told you all the news so will cease here.

Best love to all.

Les

LETTER of May 15th

Dear Mother,
Your letter of the 10th received this morning. Glad to hear you are all well, including Jack the rat-killer.[17]

I expect Dad is back from Woodford now. Hope he enjoyed his little holiday altho' on a far from pleasant errand.[18]

I got 3 letters of yours yesterday written about the 3rd week of April, no good answering those I suppose now.

We are still at the same camp; expect we shall be here for a good bit longer; it has been a very hot day, but this will be a warm hole in summer - regular "sunny France".

Shall be on the lookout for your parcel - you needn't trouble about sending any eatables - I know things are pretty short at home. We get good grub here - I just drew half a loaf as my day's bread ration.

Just had our pay - 15 francs. I don't spend much here. Only the canteen & YM to go to and they're not overstocked. I've got quite a little library of French paper money - comes in handy when I've got nothing else to read - which reminds me, if you can, do send out an occasional book or two - you know my line - for when we're out of the line and sometimes when we're in I get ample time for reading and all there is here is the Continental Daily Mail about a week old!

Yes, Armand was telling me that he might be sent out again. I very much doubt if he would get down this way as there are only a few English troops here - still you never know.

You would all enjoy the country out here, great long slopes very like the English downs. From the hill just above our camp, you have a fine view right away over the hill tops for 6 to 8 miles.

Blades' just come in, says he couldn't sit in the Y. M. any longer on account of the heat and this at 7 o'c in the evening. I reckon we shall finish off as grease spots.

That nail of mine has just started to come off; been a good old time hasn't it? I've been wearing that glove-finger this week as it keeps catching on things.

Yes, I suppose an account of our stunt[19] would be in the paper for April 27th altho' it was only a brigade attack.

William Leslie and Jack the rat killer.

Some of the undersized chaps who were kept behind when we first came out have just arrived at the camp. I suppose they'll use them for odd jobs around camp.

We have had a party of our fellows digging the camp garden for the last 2 or 3 days - reckon they want some of my carnations to smarten it up! If you're getting decent weather at home the garden should be looking well. How are those spuds - getting on that I helped to plant?

There are very little signs of war round here, no wounded or ambulances to be seen as at the old place; no sound of the guns for ever in your ears; plenty of French soldiers toddling about - good natured easy going sort they seem.

Well I think I will close now, getting on to bye bye time. I always like to lay in bed and smoke a bit - rather like Father I fancy.

Best love to all of you.

Les

Posted on 16th

P.S. I hope I'm not asking too much but can you send out 2 thin smooth material shirts - those old khaki ones of Dad's will do if he doesn't need them - these greybacks[20] *harbour vermin too much. - L*

Letter of May 17th

I received your letter of the 12th and your very welcome parcel and letter despatched on the 11th with this morning's mail.

Thank you very much for the good things in the parcel. I had quite a slap-up tea tonight - tea, bread and marmalade, nougat and cake.

Those papers came yesterday together with another letter from Armand, just a very short scrawl.

It has been very hot today, the sun seems to possess a burning quality only seldom experienced in England. I saw a party of chaps playing football tonight stripped down to the waist and really I think it would be the most comfortable attire all day.!

Yesterday we had a short route march. Started at 9.30, halted 12 - 1.30 for dinner and got back again just before 3 oc.[21]

I expect Richard will finish up in the infantry right enough, there's not much call for anything else nowadays.

Just got hold of another green envelope[16] - that makes 2. I am saving them for when we go up the line again - it's wasting them to use them now as a censored letter answers just as well here.

You see more aeroplanes at home than we do on this front. So far I've only seen one - a Fritz[22] and he was 2 or 3 miles off. There were plenty up at the last place - I saw 3 planes come down one morning - one in flames. One of our chaps was tackling a Boche[22] and they were both caught by the same shrapnel burst - nasty bump!

There is one thing here that compensates for the hot weather and that is the surprising amount of springs - you find them everywhere - I believe all the villages round here get their water from them.

Matthews heard from Lt. Collett at Dublin - he says that the yarn is round the regt that I am missing - funny how things start. You had better ask Dad to correct them when he next writes to them.

Well I think I'll close now.

Best love to all of you.

Les

Thank Auntie for cigs.

LETTER *of Sunday May 19th*

Dear Mother,

I have been expecting a letter today but nothing has arrived, only a very small mail, been held up somewhere I suppose.

Another very hot day - I have been knocking about in shirt sleeves ever since we came off parade.

I heard tonight that we are starting work at 6 a.m. so as to save working in the hottest part of the day.

Went to service this morning, very short affair as we were finished by 10.30. After that we went to the funeral of one of our chaps who died in hospital yesterday.

As I've got no letters of yours to answer I'm afraid I can't make a very long epistle of this, but I reckon to write every 2 days just to keep you posted up.

Well goodbye, love to all.

Les

Posted May 21st - no letter yet.

LETTER *of May 21st*

Dear Mother,
Recd two letters this afternoon, one of Grace's dated 14th, the other yours of the 16th. Too bad that letter of mine taking 9 days, but about that time our platoon officers were being changed and no doubt there was some delay in censoring.

Your letters are pretty regular now. I reckon on getting one practically every other day.

I expect your parcel will arrive tomorrow - am afraid I shan't want many hot drinks for the heat here is terrific - too hot to work in the middle of the day. We have reveille now at 5 a.m., first parade 6.30 and finish for the day at 11.30.

Had a good bathe tonight in a stream near the camp, pretty cold: spring water I think.

You ask if I had any livestock! Well I had a pretty good collection when I was wearing undervest and pants for the beggars stick in thick material, but now I've discarded those I think I've practically got rid of them.

Sorry to hear Charlie Goldie has been wounded but perhaps he's in Blighty by now, if so he's all right.

So Pat has gone into the infantry after all. RAF is rather a difficult thing to get in now I should think.

We were issued with short pants last night. I wish we could get khaki shorts as well. They would be fine for this weather.

Robbins has just come back from the base (where he went with a cut finger!). He says he saw Wilkins on the boat for England and he was doing well then - had one leg off. Sgt King (P.T. Inst.[23] in the N.S.Y.[24]) went with him, he lost his left arm - rather funny that the 3 P.T. men should all be hit first time - Wilkins, King and Cox.

Well I think I'll close now with very best love to all.

Les

LETTER *of May 22nd*

Dear Dad,
Many thanks for your little parcel and letter recd this morning. You see I am already using the ink.

I am enclosing with this letter a little souvenir for Grace. I hope it will arrive in time for her birthday - I got it just after we came out of the line and have carried it about ever since.

Another sweltering hot day, our attire off parade consists of a shirt and a pair of shorts and even then it's pretty warm.

I daresay I shall know Lt. Chubb when he joins us, but I can't say that I remember his name. Was he that chap who was at Oxford station when I was going back off leave?

One of our corporals was saying tonight that the Division has been in the line on our front for a fortnight and haven't had a casualty yet! Expect he was stretching it a bit. Still it's a treat to be on a quiet front after the warm time up north.

Written on the same paper,
we think on the same day, but to his mother.

I recd the "Lincs Standard" this afternoon - I was asleep at the time letters were given out and woke up to find it on the bed. You may as well put a note in the papers when you send them - there's no risk of my being charged extra postage & it's good to get a bit of handwriting from home - letters and grub are about the only things to look forward to!

I am writing this in a little wood just above our camp - I like it better than the last place - the country is a little more enclosed rather like a West Country village.

I am enclosing a letter for Wilkins' people[15]. I should think they will have heard from him by now as young Robbins saw him put on the ambulance for England at the base, maybe he has had a relapse, while in hospital at home.

Thank Dad for the cutting. It's a <u>fairly</u> accurate account of our stunt.[8]

Well, I think I'll knock off now as I've a lot more writing to do.

Best love, Les

Page 2 onwards of what appears to be another
LETTER *started on May 22nd*

This is a special reserve battalion and a good proportion of the N.C.O.s are old [Army?] men, not bad chaps in their way, but of course not of the same class as the old regts.

At present I'm in the Lewis Gun Company - rather more interesting work than in the platoon. The company is out trench digging tonight - Lewis Gunners are excused - thank goodness!

Infantry work out here is a monotonous old game - I shall try to get something more in my line soon I think - I might be able to turn my draughtsmanship to some advantage - but I don't know how to set about it!

I suppose tobacco is getting pretty dear at home. There's no shortage out here. I've got quite half a pound in an old ration bag!

May 23rd 6.30 a.m. Didn't finish this last night so thought I would carry on this morning. I am 'orderly man' today & excused parades to attend to serving the grub - bit of a change from 'orderly sgt'.

Looks like being another scorcher today - I bet when it does rain here it pours!

I don't know any of the places Mr Oliver mentions but if you draw a line from Soissons to Chateau Thierry and then select a spot 10 miles east of the centre of that line, you'll pretty well have my location!

I wrote to Sid on May 4th but haven't had an answer yet. I haven't had a letter from him all the year.

I hope you have got your meat tickets by now, no joke if you were to lose those - couldn't you make some good sandwiches with all your tickets - say a meat ticket between two bread tickets!

If ever you see a chap with a red horse shoe just below the back of his collar, you'll know he's in the 25th Division. I should say they've had as hard a time as any during the last 2 months, first on the Somme, then taken north & in retirement up there for 12 days, then we joined them and were in the counter attack on Kemmel. If the French had advanced as far as we did that morning we should have taken Kemmel all right, as it was, our right flank was in the air & Johnny started to get round us, so we had to withdraw about 400 yards to get into touch with the French.

I think our batt. took about 50 prisoners, mostly young chaps, they soon put their hands up when you showed 'em a bayonet. I 'souvenired' a good many things that day, but gave them all away as they were too much to carry about.

One thing the Boche is smart with & that is his machine guns, they were a nuisance in the last line I was in, together with a sniper. He uses his m. guns for sniping - fires a short burst whenever he detects any movement in a trench.

A German message dog[25] came into our trench the last day I was up - their sniper spotted him and killed him, but he just managed to get into our trench. He was carrying a message in German in a little can round his neck. We sent it on to B.H.Q. of course. I believe it was some instruction to one of his advanced machine gun posts with which he was mainly holding his line up there.

I got one Johnny while we were up there - sniped the beggar at 600 yards. He went down all right and then crawled into cover. I expect he's safe back in his dear old Vaderland now, thanks to me!

Well this seems to be getting a long letter, I shall get the Paper Controller after me!

Very best love to all of you.
Les

DIARY *(undated, possibly May 29th)*

The order came suddenly on Sun. evening. Parade 10.30 in battle order and we all knew there was more dirty work ahead. 10.30 saw the Company on parade ready for whatever might be doing, gas masks at the alert, haversacks in place of the valise on the back and by 11 a.m. the whole battalion was winding its way along the dusty French road towards the firing line some 10 kilometres distant.

Most of us were young chaps only a few weeks out, and although this would not be our first time "up the line" nevertheless we looked forward to the next few hours with a certain feeling of excitement for we knew that this sudden departure could only mean that Jerry was "coming over". Most of us were trying to appear unconcerned, singing the old time songs and joking about in general. After two hours of hard marching we came upon the first signs of destruction - shell holes by the roadside while here and there a roof or wall was shattered.

Soon after midnight the German barrage started and henceforth we marched amidst an inferno of sound while the summer sky was lit up in all directions by the flashes of gunfire.

Gas shells were being used in abundance and very soon our eyes were smarting and throats were dry thro' the influence of the noxious fumes that were drifting over with the breeze. Then the order was given to don respirators and for 20 minutes we marched in these, a very hot and uncomfortable time too for respirators are NOT ideal wear for a night march on a summer evening.

Field Service POSTCARD signed 'Les 29.5.18'
postmarked Army Post Office 31.5
stamped 'passed by Censor No 2432'

I have been admitted into hospital wounded and am getting on well.

Letter follows at first opportunity.

NOTHING is to be written on this side except the date and signature of the sender. Sentences not required may be erased. If anything else is added the post card will be destroyed.

~~I am quite well.~~

I have been admitted into hospital
~~sick~~ / wounded *and am going on well.* *~~and hope to be discharged soon.~~*

~~I am being sent down to the base.~~

~~I have received your~~ *~~letter dated~~* / *~~telegram ,,~~* / *~~parcel ,,~~*

Letter follows at first opportunity.

~~I have received no letter from you~~ *~~lately.~~* / *~~for a long time.~~*

Signature only. Les.

Date 29. 5. 18

[Postage must be prepaid on any letter or post card addressed to the sender of this card.]

(25350) Wt. W458-591 1,500m. 4/15 M.R.Co.,Ltd.

LETTER of May 29th from 8th Canadian Gen. Hospital,
Army P.O.S., France.
Written in pencil on scrap paper.

Dear Mother,
I expect the above address will gladden your heart. I got hit on Monday afternoon, a machine gun bullet through the right leg just above the ankle, nice cushy one eh!

I arrived here about midnight yesterday after a rather funny journey, you see we were on the Soissons front & the clearing stations[2] were being evacuated on account of our retirement & it took us an eleven hour ride in a French motor lorry to reach one that was safe - after that all was plain sailing.

I don't know yet whether we shall be sent to England as it's a long journey from here and they may decide to keep us here.

Please excuse paper but this is the only bit I had in my pockets. I lost all my kit of course.

Don't write to this address until you get my next letter.

Well, will knock off now. Am feeling all right in myself - leg aches a bit of course.

Love to all,
Les

LETTER of Thursday May 30th

Dear Mother,
I know you will be looking out for a letter from me - I couldn't get any writing paper till last night and so was only able to send you that short note.

I had a good night's sleep last night - the first since Sat. night as every night since then I have been on the move in some way or other - foot, rail & motor.

Well I suppose you'll be wanting all details as to how I got my souvenir! Of course you have seen in the papers of the heavy fighting on the Soissons front. Well we got the order on Sunday night to pack up and move off at 10 p.m. in battle order & of course we knew we were in for some more dirty work.

Army P.O.
S.5
France

8th Canadian Gen.

Dear Mother. 29.5.18

I expect the above address will gladden your heart for I got hit on Monday afternoon — a machine gun bullet thro the right leg just above the ankle nice cushy one eh.

I arrived here at about midnight yesterday after a rather funny journey. you see we were on the Soissons front & the clearing stations were being evacuated on account of our retirement & it took us an ever

We marched all night until 3 a.m. on Mon morning. Johnny had attacked at 1 a.m. after a gas shell bombardment & by using tanks had broken our front line.

We rested from about 3 a.m. until 9 a.m. in French huts about 6 kilometres behind the line and started off at 9 for the line.

When we reached there my Lewis Gun battery went into reserve trenches with 'D' Coy & we stopped in these until 2 in the afternoon when the captain thought he could find a better position for us on a rise 200 yards to our right; to get there however we had to cross a lot of ground covered by one of Jerry's machine guns & it was there that I got hit.

The first time I crossed it he dotted me one on the tin hat with a ricochet which made my head sing & then when we were returning he plugged me thro' the leg!

It felt as if somebody had hit me on the leg with a sledge hammer but didn't hurt very much. Luckily a stretcher bearer was near me & he soon tied me up & got me onto the road.

Then two chaps of the Northd. Fusiliers[26] helped me along to an ambulance about 2 kilos back along the road.

I think I was pretty near whacked when I reached it for they had to carry me the last few hundred yards.

After I got to the ambulance, they pretty soon got us down to an F.A.[27] and there about 60 of us were put in French motor lorries.

We were in these from 5 p.m. on Mon night till 3 a.m. on Tues morning & I don't want such a journey again I can tell you! for they were some shaky old crocks!

Eventually we reached a French Casualty Clearing Station where I got to bed, left again at 5 p.m. for Paris arriving here about midnight on Tues. This is a very big hospital & has, until our batch arrived, been entirely for French wounded. In our ward down one side are French & on the other English. So if I don't soon learn to speak the lingo I never shall!

The nurses and staff are all Canadian & are very good to us all. They are quite pleased to get some English tommies in at last.

Just had my wound dressed. It's quite clean; about 3 ins above the ankle, right leg, straight through bone & all, but I don't think the bone is splintered.

You'd laugh to see all the dressings I have on it; first a big wet dressing then about a square mile of oiled silk, followed by an

Canadian nurses during the First World War. Photograph courtesy of Library and Archives Canada.

enormous quantity of cotton wool; then the whole is put into a big aluminium splint to support the bone which I suppose is a bit weak, and then on top a cage to keep the bedclothes off my tootsies!

A beautiful day today. This hospital seems to be out in the country a bit altho' I couldn't see much when they brought us here from the station.

The address is simply No. 8 Canadian General Hospital, France. And by the way I am also in "France" ward.

Well, I think I'll knock off now - excuse writing but it's a bit of a job in bed.

Best love to all of you.
Les

LETTER of May 31st
(in pencil)

Dear Mother and All,
I don't know how long my letters are taking from here but expect you will get my first note from hospital soon after my letter of Sunday. I hope the enclosure arrived quite safely and that Grace will enjoy her birthday. I shall be thinking of her tomorrow.

Am going on quite well; feel absolutely fit bar my leg & that only aches slightly. It was very swollen and inflamed when I came in, but that has gone down now - Sister says I ought to give her a certificate.

Our chaps were just saying what an unlucky division ours is. We get sent to a presumably nice quiet front and lo & behold Jerry must needs start an offensive there!

No mistake, I thought I was going to be left behind once, for our chaps were retiring on all sides, but they eventually stopped and reorganised.[28]

I have been reading a terrific lot since I got here, mostly American weeklies, the only thing we can get is English papers.

The Canadian Chaplain was round here yesterday afternoon, very decent chap; he offered to write home for me but I wasn't going to trouble him to that extent.

I lost all my kit except razor, shaving brush & soap which I got a chap to take out of my pack for me; as it was I looked pretty filthy when I arrived here.

I daresay I shall land in England before long. I don't suppose they will keep us here for long while this offensive is on.

Another beautiful day, seems a shame to lie in bed & count the spots on the ceiling!

Must close in a hurry - orderly is collecting the letters.

Best love at the double to everybody.

Les

Army Form B. 104—81A.

No. ______ (If replying, please quote above No.)

Inf. Record Office Record Office.

1-1 JUN 1918 191

SIR OR MADAM,—

I regret to have to inform you that a report has been received from the War Office to the effect that (No.) 57319 (Rank) Pte (Name) W. L. Ward (Regiment) Worcestershire Regt. has been wounded, and was admitted to 8 Canadian General Hospital, St Cloud, France on the 28th day of May, 1918. The nature of the wound is Gun Shot Wound Right Leg

I am to express to you the sympathy and regret of the Army Council.

Any further information received in this office as to his condition will be at once notified to you.

Yours faithfully,

[illegible] Lieutenant

for Officer in charge of Records.

IMPORTANT.—Any change of address should be immediately notified to this Office.

NOTE (in ink) on Sunday June 2nd from Hut 13, No. 12 St Louis (U.S.A.) General Hospital, Rouen

Dear Mother,
Just a line to let you know that I arrived here at 4 a.m. this morning.

We came in a British R.C.[29] train from Paris - quite a treat after the French ones.

Was x-rayed again this afternoon to see if my leg is fractured. I will let you know the result as soon as I can.

I will write longer tomorrow - too late now.

With my best love to all.

Les

LETTER (undated but presumably Monday June 3rd)
from Rouen hospital address

Dear Mother,
I expect you will think I am dodging all over France. Never mind. I hope to dodge home very soon.

We left Paris on Saturday night at 5 p.m. by an English hospital train - quite a treat to get English grub again after French rations - too much soup for my liking!

We got into Rouen about 1 a.m. and were safely tucked into bed again by 4 o'clock - this hospital is staffed by Americans but is under British control.

I always thought American women were very tall after the Mrs Arnold style! but all the nurses here are very petite - in fact look too slight for the work.

The Yanks are fine chaps, we get them in & out all day, likewise the doctors, all young chaps.

The old leg is still going strong - gives me no pain except when I try and move it.

Just got my x-ray report. It says comminuted fracture right fibula, likewise fracture of tibia; no metal fragments - so you see I'm in for a good rest.

It's a wonder to me how I managed to walk that 2 kilometres to an ambulance - funny what you can do when Jerry's after you.

Food is fine here - actually had real butter today - makes your mouth water, eh!

I often wonder how the boys are getting on, I'm afraid they've had a rough time during the retirement. I consider I was jolly lucky to get hit the first day.

Very warm here today. I feel as if I should like all the bedclothes off!

If you do write to this address, don't put too much energy into it, as I may be moved at any time.

Well will close now.

With best love to all of you.
Les

Two CARDS *from Southampton dated 7.6.18*
one from H.M.Ship 'no charge to be raised' saying:

Arrived Southampton this morning. Cheerio. Les.

the other a Church Army card
(also marked H.M.Ship. No charge to be raised) saying:

Arrived at Southampton about six this morning, wonderfully smooth crossing from Havre. Am now on the platform waiting an ambulance train. Will write as soon as I reach hospital, Les.

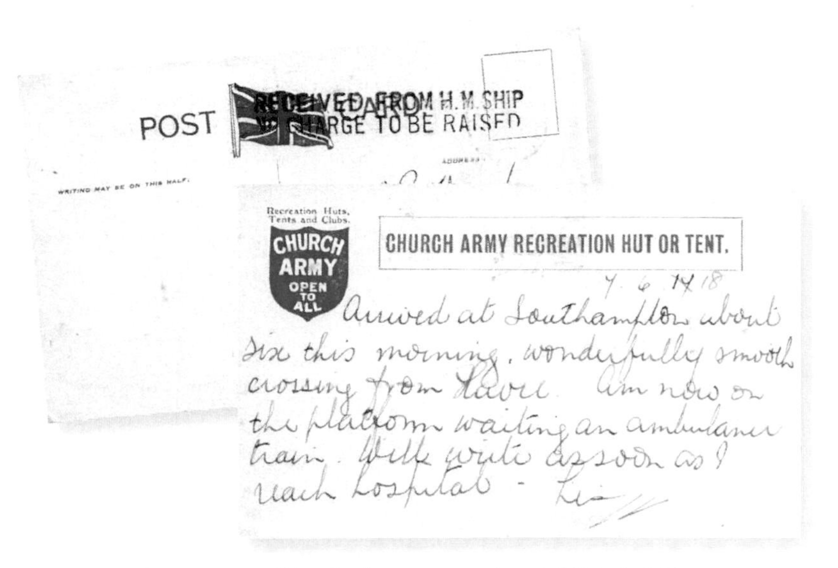
POST CARD
RECEIVED FROM H.M. SHIP
NO CHARGE TO BE RAISED

Recreation Huts, Tents and Clubs.
CHURCH ARMY
OPEN TO ALL

CHURCH ARMY RECREATION HUT OR TENT.

7. 6. 1918
Arrived at Southampton about six this morning, wonderfully smooth crossing from Havre. Am now on the platform waiting an ambulance train. Will write as soon as I reach hospital - Les

LETTER *on Church Army paper headed Ward 4 East,*
Lord Derby War Hospital, Warrington, Lancs
Sat morning (June 8th)

Dear Mother,
I expect you will have got my cards from Southampton by this morning & will be wondering where "wandering Willie" has landed.

Well, I am here! Pretty good way off isn't it? but still - I nearly got sent to Scotland!!! so ought to think myself lucky.

I daresay you would like to have an account of my journey from Rouen - well to start with, on Wed. morning the doctor marked me for "Blighty". Yes and it was a treat to see him write "England" across my card and sign it!

Our convoy left Rouen by a U.S. hospital train about 9 a.m. on Thurs. morning & arrived at Havre at about 2 p.m. I was carried straight on board the hospital ship which was the Union Castle "Grantully Castle".

I was put in my little cot. I proceeded to make myself comfortable.

We had dinner and tea on board & were then presented with a silver mounted pipe, 2 oz tobacco & 20 fags - the gift of the directors of the Union Castle line - very good weren't they?

The boat left Havre at 10 p.m. & we had a very smooth crossing - in fact you could hardly tell she was travelling.

On arriving at Southampton we had breakfast on board and were then put on board a hospital train which left S-ton about 10 a.m.

Nearly all the chaps in my carriage had their legs in splints! I lay next to a B.S.M. of the R.F.A.[30] and he was remarking what a jolly fine football team we should make.

You little thought at about 4 p.m. yesterday afternoon that your little Billy was within 400 yards of you, did you? Yet we stayed in Oxford station for about 5 mins! I felt like getting out and walking, splint and all!

Well, we eventually got here at 8.30 and I was in bed having a good supper by 9.30 - this is a fine big hospital - must have been something of the sort before the war.

I don't know whether any of you intend coming up here - if you do I should advise you to communicate with the Wesleyan Minister here as this hospital is 3 or 4 miles from Warrington itself & perhaps he could tell you what to do with regard to accommodation.

I couldn't see much of the place when we came in - being a stretcher case, but it seemed to be a pretty spot quite away from all the smoke and dirt of the factories.

I'm enclosing a 5 Fr. note. I believe you could change it at the General P.O., you can use the proceeds in buying 1½d stamps - otherwise you'll get no letters! as I have no English money (you should get at least 3s 4d for 5 Fr.)

Another thing I want is writing paper - I'm afraid some fat old German is using my writing pad, likewise the rest of my kit.

Don't forget when you do write that I've had no letter since I was hit, so shall expect all the news (if you can't put it in a letter, make a parcel of it!)

Shall have to knock off now, no more paper.

With very best love to all.

Les

Leg going on A1.

Some items that William Leslie kept with the letters:

Right: a tobacco box sent to troops by Princess Mary intended for Christmas 1914. Due to a shortage of brass, some of the last ones went out in 1919. Mary was the 17-year-old daughter of King George V and Queen Mary.

Right: 10th Hussars collar badge from the kit of Capt. Mills (W.L.'s fathers's 3rd Dragoon Guards friend). Mills died of his wounds in 1918.

Bottom right: a German Iron Cross, probably brought back from France in the kit of Lt. L.A. Hartshorn, who died of his wounds in March 1918. Laurie Hartshorn was the brother of Gladys, whom my father later married.

Below: mock Iron Cross produced in England to ironically celebrate German 'atrocity' attacks on various towns. Scarborough, Whitby and Hartlepools were shelled from the sea in the winter of 1914.

Army Form B. 2079.

Serial No. 4473 Yor Destroct

NOTE—This Certificate is to be issued without any alterations in the manuscript

Certificate of discharge of No. 37319 Rank Private

Name Ward (Surname) William Leslie (Christian Names in full)

Unit* and Regiment or Corps from which discharged: Worcestershire Regt

*The unit of the Regiment or Corps such as Field Co. R.E., H.T. or M.T., A.S.C., etc., is invariably to be stated.

Regiment or Corps to which first posted 2 OX A

Also previously served in O B L I

Worc Regt

Oxford

±60518.35

Only Regiments or Corps in which the soldier served since August 4th, 1914, are to be stated. If inapplicable this space is to be ruled through in ink and initialled.

Specialist Qualifications (Military) Nil Chm (one Blue)

Medals, Clasps, Decorations and Mentions in dispatches: Nil

Wound Stripes* One (To be inserted in words)

Has served Overseas on Active Service†

Enlisted at Oxford on 7 Dec 1916

*Each space is to be filled in and the word "nil" inserted where necessary.
†To be struck out in ink if not applicable.

He is discharged in consequence of Being no Longer Physically fit for War Service Para 392 (XVI) KR

after serving* one years* 353 days with the Colours, and — years* — days in the Army Reserve or Territorial Force† (Strike out whichever inapplicable)

* Each space is to be filled in and the word "nil" inserted where necessary; number of years to be written in words.
†Service with Territorial Force to be shown only in cases of soldiers serving on a T.F. attestation.

Date of discharge 29 1 19

Signature and Rank. J. Downs 2 Lt

Officer i/c Records.

Warwick (Place).

Description of the above-named soldier when he left the Colours.

Year of Birth 1899

Marks or Scars Wd Scar above Rt Ankle

Height 5 ft. 9 in.

Complexion Fresh

Eyes Brown Hair Black

[P.T.O.

(A11039) Wt.W1912/PP1138. 240,000 6/18. Sch. 44. D. D. & L.

WARNING.—If this Certificate is lost a duplicate cannot be issued. You should therefore on no account part with it or forward it by post when applying for a situation.

GEORGIVS V BRITT: OMN: REX ET IND: IMP:

FOR LONG SERVICE AND GOOD CONDUCT

1914 1918

THE GREAT WAR FOR CIVILISATION 1914-1919

CHAPTER 4

After the War

THE PEACE arrangements were hammered out at Versailles in 1919. The French and some of the British wanted to impose tough conditions on Germany. A large bill for reparations was drawn up; Alsace and Lorraine (which Germany had taken from France in 1870) were returned to France; the German fleet was handed over to Britain (and scuppered at Scapa Flow); German military expenditure was to be strictly limited; the Rhineland was to be demilitarised and occupied by the Allies for 15 years. Germany lost her colonies: German South West Africa eventually became the independent state of Namibia; German East Africa, with Zanzibar, became the present day Tanzania. The German peace treaty with Russia was revoked and Poland made wholly independent (since 1815 she had been under Russian sovereignty).

President Wilson of America played a prominent part in the negotiations, emphasising particularly the principle of 'self-determination'. The Austro-Hungarian Empire was broken up into a small Austria and a separate Hungary; Czechs and Slovaks were joined in Czechoslovakia (they separated in 1993); Serbia and adjacent countries were formed into Yugoslavia (which was broken up in 2006). President Wilson was also a prime mover in the formation of the League of Nations to which international disputes were to be referred (though sadly America did not become a member).

★ ★ ★

Standing left to right: Armand, Grace, Dorothy, my father William Leslie. Seated: my grandmother, Grace Amelia, and grandfather, William Robert Ward.

After he left the Army in 1918, my father's father, William Robert Ward, worked with the Oxford branch of the Ministry of Pensions and the family moved to 24 Beechcroft Road in north Oxford. In 1924 he retired and moved to Essex, first to Danbury where he had a smallholding and then to Rayleigh where he died in 1934. His wife, my grandmother, died in 1945. Grace, my father's older sister, married Armand (mentioned in the letters from France) in 1921. They had five children - Kingsley (1924), Frances (1927), Roger (1930), Graham (1936) and Sheila (1942). Father also had a younger sister Dorothy (Doff) who married in 1938. She had two children, Mary (1939) and David (1942).

My father returned from France to pursue a career as an architect, as he tells us in his memoirs.

> *After spending several months in the Oxford Workhouse which had become an auxiliary to the main General Hospital in the Examination Schools, I filled up my own demob' papers, went before a medical board which gave me a 20 per cent disability pension and returned to Canal House to*

consider the future. It was now January 1919 and authority had begun to think what had to be done to redeem the promise of a 'land fit for heroes' (I never heard of that at the time).

At the end of the war an organisation had been set up known as 'The Appointments Department'. Its function was to assist ex-servicemen whose education or training had been interrupted by their war service.

I went along to the Oxford branch which was mainly staffed by junior officers awaiting demobilisation. They politely enquired what I wanted and I told them 'training for a career'. Here I think some explanation is necessary. I regarded my filling of Father's post for over two years as a wartime stopgap undertaken to release an experienced soldier for training purposes. That before then I had been a junior clerk I chose to ignore for I soon realised I could do better than that and in any case it was not a job of my seeking. And so when I filled up my papers before discharge, I had inserted under the heading 'Previous occupation' the description 'schoolboy'. I do not think that anyone has been harmed by the falsehood. Or is that too Jesuitical a view?

He looked at my demob papers and said, "Yes, that's right. It says 'schoolboy'. What do you want to do?" I said, "Well, I am rather inclined to think architecture!" He looked a bit blank and I think one of them did not know how to pronounce the word. Anyway they looked up their files and said, "You can either go to one of the architectural schools in Birmingham or Liverpool or we have three letters from practising architects who are prepared to take ex-servicemen as articled pupils!" Well, after four years of rather stop-gap work I didn't really want to begin studying pure and simple, I wanted to get down to work and I said I would rather go into the office of a practising architect. "All right," they said, "we'll send off telegrams to these three architects and will let you know the result." Within a few days I was informed that a Burton-on-Trent architect had been the first to reply and that he had confirmed that he was willing to take an ex-serviceman as a pupil.

So, somewhere about March 1919 I reported at Burton-on-Trent. I'd been given a full pension to tide me over before a final grant was settled. This was somewhere in the order of 35/- a week. So I settled down to three years training as an articled pupil.

It was at this firm of architects in Burton-on-Trent that he met my mother, Gladys Hartshorn. They married in 1924. He served as an architect with the London County Council from then until he retired in 1958. He joined the Auxiliary Airforce (balloon barrage) during the Second World War, being released 'at his own request' in 1943 to help with post-war LCC housing plans. He was much involved with the building of 'out-county' housing estates such as Harold Hill and Sheerwater. For many years he was Secretary of the Trustees of Epsom Methodist Church for which he designed a new Hall and Church Lobby. He died in 1974. My mother had died nearly ten years earlier. They had four children - John (1926), myself Alec (1928), Michael (1930) and Christopher (1935).

Left: Gladys Hartshorn.

Opposite: Gladys with my father, William Leslie.

Above: the Ward family home at Hessle Grove, Ewell, designed by William Leslie.

Right: the family at home in Ewell.

Left: William Leslie on Streatham Common during service with the Auxiliary Air force during the Second World war.

Far Left: service medals from 1945.

D.L.Macintyre Esq.,
The Establishment Section,
Secretariat,
H.M.Office of Works,
WESTMINSTER, S.W.I.

January 8th.1925.

Sir,

I should be very much obliged if you would kindly consider my name for employment as an Architectural Assistant. I give particulars of my Military Service and Qualifications below:-

NAME............. William Leslie Ward.

AGE.............. 24 years.

ADDRESS.......... 95 Moor Street,BURTON-ON-TRENT.

MILITARY SERVICE. Enlisted at the age of Eighteen. Served for a period of two years in England,Ireland and France with the Queen's Own Oxfordshire Hussars,the Oxford and Bucks Light Infantry and the Worcestershire Regiment. Severely wounded in May,1918,and after eight months in hospital discharged as unfit for further service, since then recovered from disability

TRAINED UNDER THE APPOINTMENTS DEPARTMENT SCHEME FOR EX-SERVICE MEN. ARTICLES served with Mr.Thomas Jenkins,J.P.,Licentiate R.I.B.A., Architect and Surveyor,Arcade Buildings,Station Street,Burton-on-Trent, and since retained by him as an Assistant.
Four years experience in one of the busiest practices of the Midlands. Including experience in the design and supervision in building of:-

Schools.	Residences.
Hospitals.	Public Houses.
Kinemas.	Factories,
Brewery Buildings.	Shops.
State-Aided Housing.	Memorials,etc,etc.

Surveying of all kinds.
Levelling.
Dilapidations (for Marquis of Anglesey and others)
Specifications.
Mining Subsidence work
Valuations for Insurance.
Quantities.
Perspectives in colour and Black and White.
Reports and Surveys illustrated by photographs.

CLERK OF THE WORKS to the Repton Rural District Council during the construction of 80 Houses on Nine separate Sites, including measuring up and handling of Builders' Final Accounts for a total of £80,000.

I am accustomed to carry the working drawings of a job right through from a rough sketch,preparing all details etc.

Present Salary..... £4-0-0.per week (Note' this is in provinces)

Specimens of work produced as desired. Free on receipt of a weeks notice.

Yours respectfully,

C. V. of William Leslie.

TO WHOM IT MAY CONCERN.

I am advised that Mr.W.L.Ward is an applicant for the post of Assistant Architect and I have pleasure in testifying as to his character and the ability he has displayed during my offical connection with him.

During the past three years Mr.Ward has acted,either jointly or solely,as Clerk of the Works to the Repton Rural District Council,under the supervision of Mr.Thomas Jenkins,the Council's Architect,and has been engaged in the supervision of the several Housing Schemes carried out by my Authority.

Mr.Ward has always performed the duties of his office with marked ability and expedition,and gave entire satisfaction to my Council whilst supervising the Housing Schemes in question,and I have no hesitation in recommending him for the appointment for which he is now an applicant.

Since the actual completion of the building,some six months ago, Mr.Ward has been engaged in the checking of the Contractor's Final Accounts,which has undoubtedly proved of great use to him as an experience in this class of work owing to the fact that they were very intricate.

I can also speak very highly of Mr.Ward's personal character and I am sure that if he is honoured with the appointment he will give the utmost satisfaction.

Dated this 13th.day of December,1922.

(Signed) H.S.Askew,

CLERK TO THE REPTON RURAL DISTRICT COUNCIL.

Reference from Repton Rural District Council.

Above: office gang May 1936. William Leslie seated second from left.

ROUND THE DEPARTMENTS

ARCHITECT'S

Mr W. L. Ward, A.R.I.B.A.

CAN'T AFFORD LIFE ASSURANCE?

In these costly times it's a work of art to balance the family budget, but Life Assurance is a MUST and need not be costly.

If you have a mortgage, a Mortgage Protection Policy to cover this costs only 4/9d. a month at age of 30 for each £1,000.

Or you can insure an income of £150 per year for your family in the event of your death, payable for 30 years, for only 16/2d. a month.

QUOTATIONS FOR ALL AGES AND ALL TERMS

For full particulars, write, 'phone or call:—

MECCA (BROKERS) LTD.

217, Westminster Bridge Road, S.E.1

Tel. WAT 6075 OPPOSITE COUNTY HALL

CHIEF ENGINEER'S

310 NOVEMBER 1958

Left: London County Council Staff Gazette, November 1958, on his retirement.

Left to right: the Ward boys, Christopher, Alec, Michael and John.

William Leslie.

The Aisne in 2008 . . .

Above: the field where William Leslie was shot, between the river and canal, viewed from Concevreux. In the foreground is the Aisne canal - the disused bridge over the river can just be seen amongst the trees in the middle left of the picture. The village of Chaudardes is in the background.

Above: the bridge over the Aisne canal with Concevreux in the background.

Right: William Leslie's granddaughter Rosie Ward-Allen and great granddaughters Grace Amelia and Constance Isobel by the Aisne at Maizy.

W. L. Ward's Family Tree

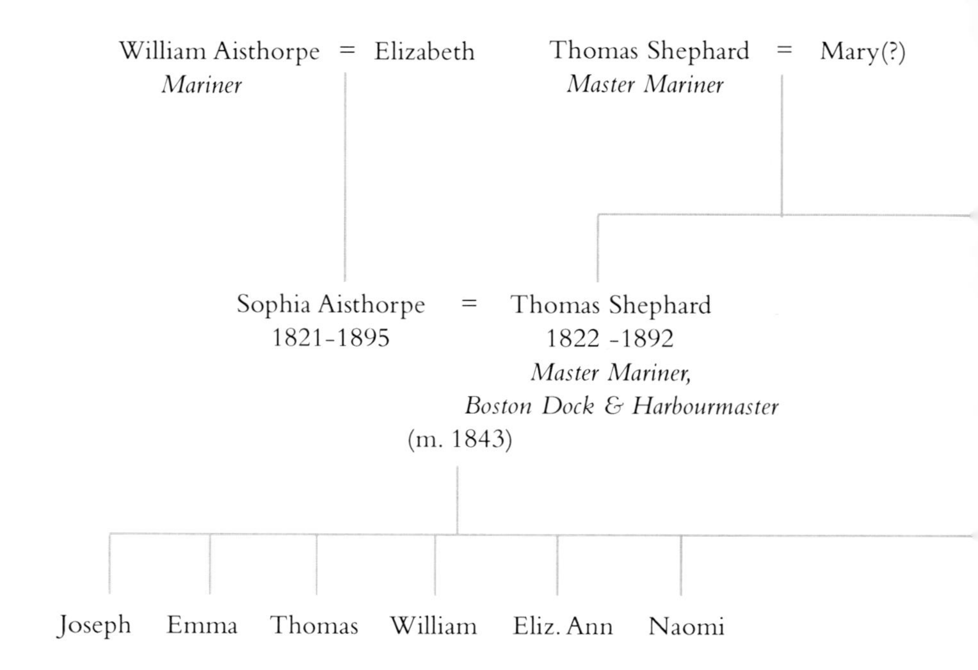

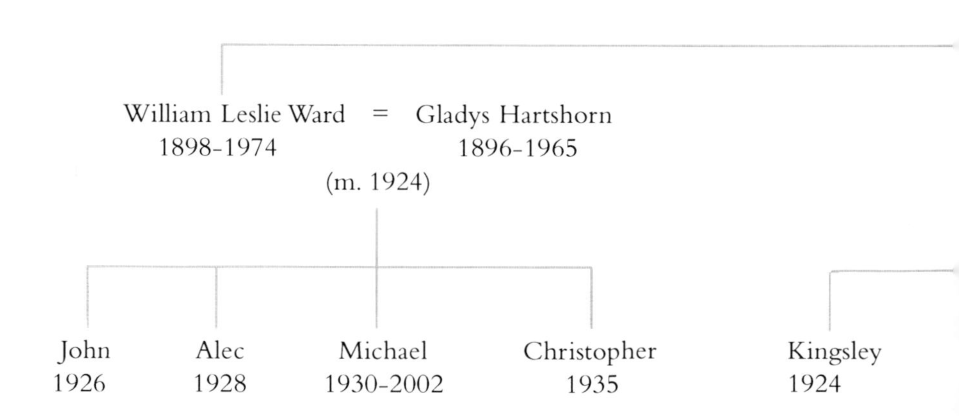

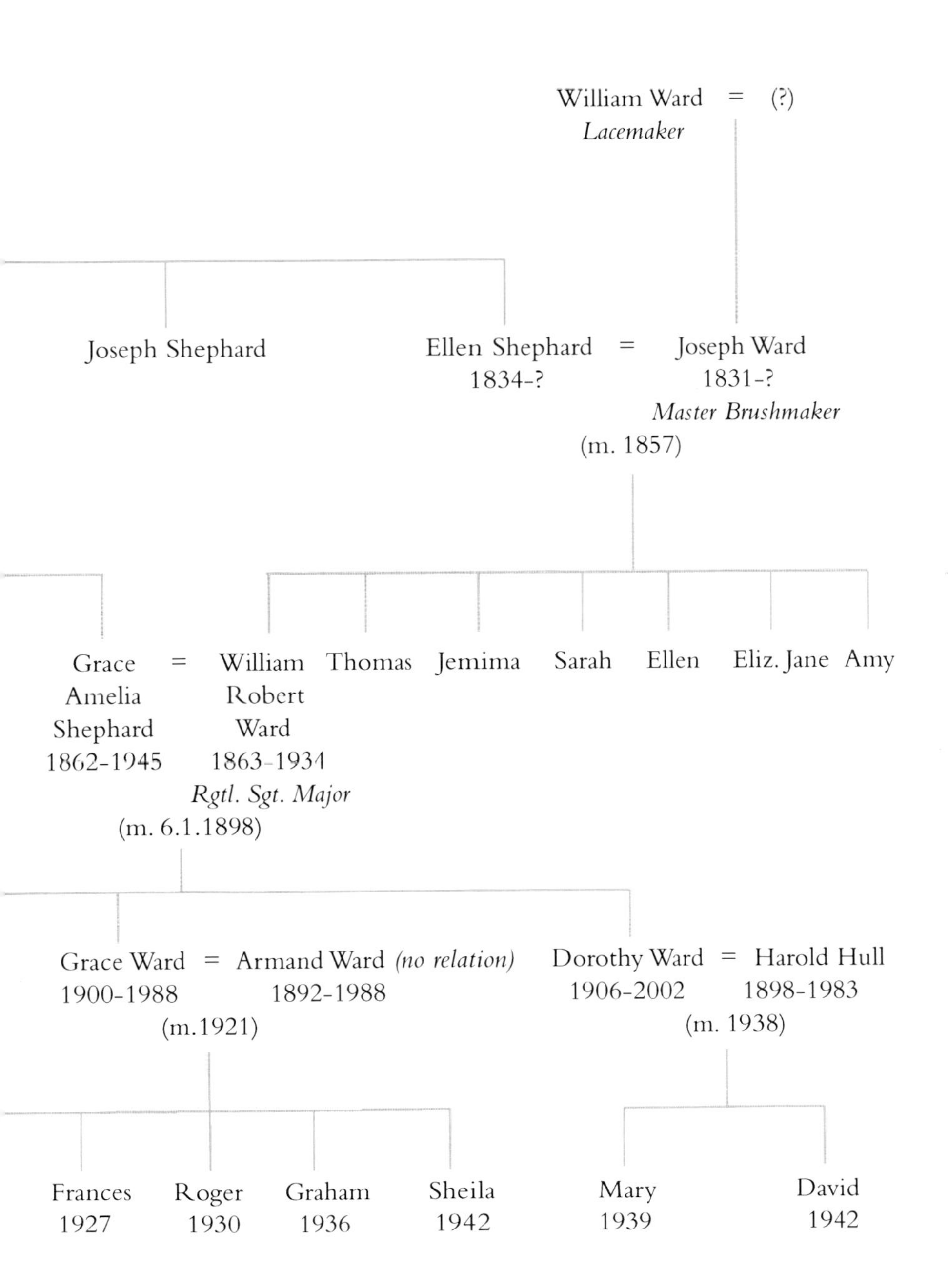
William Ward = (?)
Lacemaker
Joseph Shephard
Ellen Shephard = Joseph Ward
1834-?
1831-?
Master Brushmaker
(m. 1857)
Grace Amelia Shephard
1862-1945
=
William Robert Ward
1863-1931
Rgtl. Sgt. Major
(m. 6.1.1898)
Thomas
Jemima
Sarah
Ellen
Eliz. Jane
Amy
Grace Ward = Armand Ward (no relation)
1900-1988
1892-1988
(m.1921)
Dorothy Ward = Harold Hull
1906-2002
1898-1983
(m. 1938)
Frances 1927
Roger 1930
Graham 1936
Sheila 1942
Mary 1939
David 1942

Germans advancing across the Aisne battlefield 1918. Courtesy of the Imperial War Museum.

APPENDIX 1

The Battle of the Aisne 1918

My father, William Leslie, was in the Oxford Yeomanry who were then attached to the Royal Worcestershires to join the 25th Division in France. One of the books that he kept in his library, and which he had annotated, was a book produced for the 25th Division, written by Lieutenant Colonel M. Kincaid-Smith in 1918. On the end-paper my father wrote:

W. L. Ward
57319
3rd Battalion Worcesters
74 Brigade
25 Division

The following is an extract from that book which covers the day on which my father was shot, 27th May 1918.

THE 25TH DIVISION IN FRANCE AND FLANDERS
BATTLE OF THE AISNE, 27TH MAY 1918

The 9th of May, the 25th Division entrained at Rexpoede and other small sidings N. W. of Poperinghe, and commenced its long journey of about thirty hours to the district near Fismes, about 20 miles S. E. of Soissons in Champagne. Here the Division learned that it once more came under the leadership of the IXth Corps.

To the few in the 25th Division who had served with the original British Expeditionary Force in August and September 1914, the district brought memories of the Battle of the Marne and the subsequent advance to the Aisne; but no hint was given of the extent of the tragedy shortly to be enacted over this historic ground.

The 50th, 8th, and 21st Divisions had all reached the new area a few days previous to the arrival of the 25th Division and were gradually relieving French Divisions of the VIth French Army, in the sector east of the Chemin des Dames and on both banks of the Aisne. All four Divisions had recently been engaged in the fighting, both in Flanders and on the Somme, from the commencement of the great German offensive and all were urgently in need of a period of training or at any rate the opportunity to recuperate in a quiet sector of the line before taking part in any further fighting. This rest was promised to the troops in the sector east of Craonne, now taken over by the IXth Corps. Very little artillery activity was displayed by either side and the troops both on the British and the neighbouring French front appeared to have settled down to a period of peaceful trench warfare.

The front, of about 24,000 yards, held by the IXth British Corps ran along the high ground about four miles north of the Aisne for the first 16,000 yards, gradually bending back S. E. on its right to the important point of Berry-au-Bac, where the line crossed the river and continued on S. E. in the direction of Rheims for another 8,000 yards.

The right sector, south of the Aisne, was held by the 21st Division, in touch with the 36th French Division on its right; the 8th Division in the centre, and the 50th Division to the left, joining up with the 22nd French Division of the XIth French Corps, north of Craonne. From this point the French front lay along the important and commanding ridge known as the Chemin des Dames, captured by the French troops in April 1917.

Whether the subsequent attack on 27th May was part of a deliberate policy to attack and destroy exhausted British Divisions in whatever sector of the line they might be found, or whether these sectors were chosen for attack irrespective of their defenders, is a point known only to the Germans themselves. But there is no doubt that these few British Divisions, in their exhausted, untrained and unwelded state, both out-numbered, out-gunned, and practically unprovided with aeroplanes, were totally unable to withstand the shock of the German assaults and successfully defend the sector of the line assigned to them along the Aisne.

Divisional headquarters were established at Arcis-le-Ponsart . . . The weather was glorious, and this famous district of Champagne, with its steep valleys and wooded hillsides, was looking at its very best and provided a pleasant change after the flat and dull monotony of Flanders. Billets were scarce, but the troops of the Division found ample and extremely comfortable accommodation in the very excellent hutted camps erected by the French in their back areas. All units at once settled down to a good three weeks training, and events, it was hoped, would allow of sufficient time to train and absorb the reinforcements who were daily arriving in large numbers for the Division . . .

The 25th Division, during the battle of the Lys and the fighting around Kemmel, between 9th April and 4th May, had lost over 7,000 men or two-thirds of its fighting strength, including no less than nine of its commanding officers and 275 other officers. These heavy losses, coming on top of the casualties sustained by the Division in the battle of Bapaume between 21st and 26th March (175 officers and 3,179 other ranks), made it imperative in the interests of the fighting efficiency of the Division for the new commanding officers and the large number of junior officers to have suitable opportunity to get an intimate knowledge of their men before taking part in any further fighting.

It had been abundantly proved during the recent battle, that the units with their abnormal proportion of boys under 20 years of age and older men over 35 were not up to the previous standard. The scarcity of men of the best fighting ages between 21 and 28 was most noticeable in every unit.

About the middle of May reports were received from escaped French prisoners that immense dumps of ammunition had been formed behind the German front, telephone cable and field guns dug in; all of which went to prove that the enemy were making deliberate preparations for an attack, although there was no sign of any concentration of troops . . . The afternoon of 26th May, definite information was received that the enemy intended to deliver an attack the following morning on both the French front along the Chemin des Dames, and that of the British IXth Corps, and possibly the French front on our right . . .

At 1 a.m., 27th May, the Germans commenced a heavy bombardment with gas shells of every description and H.E.[31]

The villages in the back areas as far as Fismes, as well as the front and support lines were deluged with shells from upwards of a thousand guns, to which we were able to reply with four Divisional Artillerys, totally 144 field guns and 48 howitzers and 118 medium and heavies, chiefly French. A very inadequate supply of gas shells was available with which to reply to the enemy's intense bombardment. This lasted to 4 a.m. when the German infantry delivered their attack.

The artillery bombardment was accompanied by an intense trench mortar bombardment. The great development of this weapon by the Germans in range, accuracy and portability has undoubtedly provided an effective answer to the elaborate and well-wired system of trenches on which both sides have been accustomed to rely. These trench mortars, used in large numbers, are able to blow away with equal ease thick or narrow belts of wire and render any trench system within their range quite untenable. Fire trenches and communication trenches are blown in; all movement or reinforcement of the men in the bombarded zone is quite impossible and the troops holding these lines whether in small or large numbers, are practically destroyed or so dazed that there can be no effective resistance to any subsequent infantry attack. The most effective reply to these hurricane trench mortar bombardments undoubtedly consists in a withdrawal just before the attack from the front system of defence to a main battle line at least two miles behind, leaving only a thin line of outposts in the original front line . . .

Five German Divisions . . . took part in the assault of the IXth Corps front . . . Thirteen German Divisions, with another eight Divisions behind, were employed against the French front of about 30 miles . . . the German advance was so rapid that by 8 a.m. the whole of the 50th and 8th Divisional Artillery north of the Aisne was in their hands and a little later half of that of the 25th Division. The battalions holding the front line were swept away and the remnants falling back on the river.

The 25th Division, which was in Corps reserve, was instructed to hold the second line of defence south of the Aisne along the heights south of the Maizy-Cormicy Road, thence bending back south-east to Trigny, a line of about 12 miles; at the same time sending one battalion forward to guard the bridges between

Concevreux and Pontavert . . . [but] the enemy were across the canal before the battalion could get into position . . .

By mid-day the Germans had succeeded in crossing the river and canal both at Maizy on our left and at Pontavert, in front of the centre of our position, their advance being facilitated by the failure to destroy the bridges. On the left, the 74th Brigade were unable to gain touch with the French troops who had fallen back south of the river, and a gap of about two miles was left practically undefended between Maizy and the French right at Villers-en-Prayeres.

Early in the afternoon, 100 men of the 74th Brigade Instructional Platoon . . . were sent forward to help fill the gap. When approaching Glennes, they encountered the enemy in large numbers. The platoon, a body of picked men, fought most gallantly against overwhelming odds and succeeded in delaying the enemy's advance for over an hour. Ultimately, after the majority had become casualties, the remainder, when nearly surrounded, were forced to retire, and only one officer and two men succeeded in rejoining the Brigade.

At about three in the afternoon the enemy, who had crossed the river and canal at Maizy, were reported to be advancing in force down the valley towards Muscourt, and in addition large bodies were seen coming from the direction of Pontavert. The attack developed along the line between 3 and 4 p.m. . . .

During their retirement the 3rd Worcesters suffered heavily . . . Before dark the line gradually retired to new positions about 1½ miles north of Romain . . .

It is difficult to write of the events of the 27th May, with reserve. The three Brigades of the 25th Division were placed by the IXth Corps, early in the fight, under the command of the 21st, 8th and 50th Divisions; no reserves of either infantry or artillery were kept in hand, whilst a big gap of at least two miles was left undefended between the 74th Brigade and the right flank of the XIth French Corps. The 50th and 8th Divisions were practically destroyed before 8 a.m. in their positions on the north of the Aisne, and but few managed to escape across the river. Important bridges at Pontavert, Concevreux and to the west of Maizy were not blown up, allowing the enemy to cross the river without difficulty. Expected to check an enemy flushed with initial success, and overwhelming in numbers, the 25th Division never had the remotest chance of holding the German division for any appreciable time, over the wide stretches of country between the right of the XIth French Corps and the 21st Division.

Enemy aeroplanes during the whole day were able to fly low and observe every movement of the British troops, guide the attacking infantry and direct the German artillery fire and themselves attack our infantry with bombs and machine guns. There was no gun of any description behind our Brigades with which to reply . . .

The Germans employed the same methods as had proved so successful up north during their attacks. After their capture of our system of defence, the advance was made by trickling forward all along the front with small columns which wormed their way through cover and folds in the ground with great skill, and, what is perhaps more important, with great determination. These small columns were invariably accompanied by light machine guns, which were used with great skill. Also, during the attack, these light machine guns were usually used to cover the short rushes forward of each group of men, and proved most successful in obtaining a superiority in the volume of fire, whilst the infantry whom they were covering were getting forward. To their skill in the employment of the light machine gun must be attributed a large share of the German success.

For those of us fortunate enough not to have experienced war, the horrors are unimaginable. Sidney Rogerson's book The Last of the Ebb, *1937, leaves us in no doubt of what it felt like to be on the front line in the First World War and an extract from his book is reproduced here with the kind permission of the publishers of the 2007 edition, Greenhill Books, London. Sidney Rogerson was commissioned straight from Cambridge University Officers' Training Corps into the West Yorkshire Regiment. After the First World War, he worked for the War Office, at the personal request of Winston Churchill. He was the author of six books, including* Twelve Days on the Somme.

THE LAST OF THE EBB, SIDNEY ROGERSON 1937

. . . the battles of the Somme, Pashendaele, Loos or Neuve Chappelle . . . are common currency among the general reading public. Moreover, they are all actions which were fought in more or less the same circumstances and surroundings: the mud, the barbed wire, the high explosives, the trenches, pill-boxes, and all the stock-in-trade of the scene-painter of the World War. The battle of the Aisne was something different, just as it was more immediately successful from the enemy's point of view and more disastrous from the point of view of the French and British. At no other time was a British army corps so nearly annihilated as was the IXth Corps between the Aisne and Marne in May 1918. Fighting under French command, inadequately supported by artillery and practically without help from the air, the four tired divisions were forced to fight and run, fight and walk, twenty-seven miles in four days across wooded downlands and three fair rivers, in brilliant summer weather and subsisting on a mixture of hard emergency rations and the good wine of Champagne. It was an astonishing battle in a novel setting, and it contained many notable feats of arms. It should therefore be better known.

. . . If for us the battle was the last of the ebb, for the Germans it was the top of the flow, a spring tide the tactical success of which was the measure of its strategic failure. . . That there was a sudden change in the German plan . . . [Is] clear. The original intention was to attack on a narrow front and with limited objectives so as to engage the Allies and prevent them from interfering with German plans elsewhere, but the astonishing success of their breakthrough persuaded the High Command, I cannot help thinking against their better judgement, to make a gambler's drive for Paris and to lose all . . .

The first news of this [impending German attack] reached us about 3.45 p.m. on May 26. In a shallow trench outside the mess dug-out, Millis and I were stretching ourselves in the sun. A signaller came up and handed Millis the little pink telephone slip. He read it and without a word passed it to me. "The enemy will attack on a wide front at 01.00 hours tomorrow, 27th inst.: A.A.A." - then followed orders for taking up battle stations.

For a second we looked at each other in silence. In a flash the whole world had changed. The landscape around us smiled no longer. It was all a grinning reality, a mockery designed to raise our hopes so they could be shattered the more pitilessly. The sun still blazed down but it had lost its heat. Millis said something like, "Oh, well, it can't be helped. We're for it again," and went off to break the news to the General.

So the blow had fallen. For the third time we were to bear the brunt of an enemy offensive. Surely we who had suffered so much already might have been spared this! It was too much to hope that those of us who had come through so far would again escape . . .

It was a splendid evening, as the sun waned and we stood on our hillock waiting for dinner we looked down on the scene around us, across the green shrubbery where the smoke from the Middlesex cook-houses rose in thin blue pillars through the still air, and over to the trees and reeds that marked the course of the Aisne River. It was all so peaceful and so vibrant with life, yet by tomorrow's light what would have happened? High overhead, mere black spots in the soft amber haze were two German planes quartering the ground like hovering kestrels and noting every moment of the tiny mice below. Not a gun fired at them, nor friendly aeroplane went to drive them off, for the French, it seemed, had neither "Archies" nor aircraft available. For the first time in the war I had the feeling that there was no one behind us, no help which could be relied upon in case of need to stem a breach or retake a vital point.

. . . How that evening dragged! The minutes crept slowly toward zero hour . . . I had gone into the mess to inquire from Johns, our imperturbable mess-corporal, whether he was all packed-up ready to move if necessary. I took a whisky-and-soda and was standing talking to him when suddenly whizz - plop! whizz - plop! Two German gas shells burst close at hand, punctual heralds of the storm. Within a second a thousand guns roared out their iron hurricane. The night was rent with sheets of flame. The earth shuddered under the avalanche of missiles: leapt skywards in dust and tumult. Ever above the din screamed the fierce crescendo of approaching shells, ear-splitting crashes as they burst: all the time the dull thud, thud, thud of detonations - drumfire . . . Inferno raged and whirled around the Bois des Buttes. The dug-outs rocked, filled with the acrid fumes of cordite, the sickly-sweet tang of gas. Timbers started. Earth showered from the roof. Men rushed for shelter, seizing kits, weapons, gas-masks, message pads as they dived for safety. It was a descent into hell. Crowded with jostling, sweating humanity, the deep dug-outs reeked, and to make matters worse, we had no sooner got below than gas began to filter down. Gas masks were hurriedly donned and anti-gas precautions taken . . . Mercifully that night was short in time however long it seemed, otherwise we could not have endured, crammed as we were into stinking, overcrowded holes, forty feet below ground, all the entrances sealed up and charcoal braziers burning, heaving to get a breath of oxygen through the gas-mask with its clip on nostrils and its gag between teeth . . .

Dawn began to break outside, but no news reached us that the enemy had yet attacked . . . The thump! - thud! - thump! - thud! overhead told us the barrage continued . . . at about 5.30 a.m. - the left flank brigade, 149th, reported, "Enemy has broken our battle-line and is advancing on Ville au Bois."

Before a word had come that our front had been assaulted, the enemy had turned both flanks and were closing on the Bois des Buttes . . . Our position was no longer a stronghold but a death-trap. There was nothing left but to obey orders and fall back across the Aisne - a decision no sooner taken than acted upon. Men struggled into their battle equipment as they clambered up the steep stairs, abandoning everything except the office confidential dispatch-box . . .

What a scene met us as we floundered into the light of the young day! Everywhere was ruin, desolation thinly veiled by mist and smoke. The barrage had begun to lift a little but was still very heavy, and the line of the Aisne spouted black where big shells were bursting. The party stood about uncertain which way to take. "Rogerson," the Brigadier yelled above the racket, "you know the way to the trench, don't you? Well, lead on!"

Wanting no second bidding, I put my head down - the instinctive action of a man fronting a storm - and dashed off into the whirling cordite dust which filled the trench. The goggles of my gas-mask fogged before I had run twenty yards. I collided violently with the trench wall, turned to see how the others were following - and found I was alone! Then did Terror, which had been dogging my thoughts since the afternoon before, take hold of me. At any second one of those screaming missiles might rend me, stretch me bleeding but conscious on the battered earth, where I should lie till Death or a not-too-kindly enemy should find me. My fear in that moment was not of death but of disablement ... To share danger with others was bearable, to be alone was terrifying.

APPENDIX 2

W. L. Ward's Probable Journey Through France

April 1918

13th - Boulogne and from there to Etaples (camp)
15th - Saint Marie Cappel (camp)
21st - Popperinge (camp)
25th - Kemmel (front line)
27th - withdrawn to reserve lines
30th - Kemmel (front line)

May 1918

2nd - withdrawn to reserve lines
7th - Wormhoudt (camp)
8th - Rexpoede (train to camp)
10th - Fere-en-tardenois (camp)
23rd - north to Vesles river (camp)
26th - north to Concevreux
27th - wounded and taken south to Marne Field Hospital
28th - Paris (hospital)

June 1918

2nd - Rouen (hospital)
7th - Le Havre - Southampton

Footnotes

1. A basic rail carriage.

2. Clearing Stations were makeshift 'hospitals' behind the lines where emergency surgery could be carried out. They were the second port of call for casualties after they had left the Field Ambulances.

3. After recruitment, soldiers were divided into categories based on physical fitness and training levels. A was 'fit for service', A2 was similar but with lower levels of training.

4. Oxford and Bucks Light Infantry.

5. Draft Commanding Officer.

6. Wivenhoe - where his regiment had been stationed in the Park under canvas in 1917 - is now the site of Essex University.

7. Company.

8. Kemmel, south-west of Ypres.

9. I have been unable to find a definition for K.D. in this context.

10. Armand was the boyfriend of my father's sister Grace.

11. Wormoudt, northern France.

12. Expeditionary Force.

13. Fere-en-Tardenois, south of the Aisne.

14. Given to him by his regiment on his retirement.

15. Although my father says here that he has heard Wilkins has died, it seems this was not confirmed in letters he received from England and without this confirmation he assumes, as later letters show, that Wilkins may still be alive in a UK hospital. The roll of honours of the 3rd Worcester Regiment include one Sergeant Frederick Albert Wilkins who died of wounds in 'France and Flanders' on 26th April, 1918 but there is no evidence that would confirm this to be the same Wilkins.

16. Letters sent in green envelopes were not censored in the sender's unit although they were subject to discretionary censorship at base. They were rationed amongst soldiers but it seems they were often traded for other items.

17. The family dog.

18. There were family connections in Woodford - my grandparents were married there - and we assume that the 'far from pleasant errand' must refer to a family bereavement.

19. He refers here to the offensive action at Kemmel.

20. Greybacks were army-issue shirts for 'other' ranks.

21. 3 o'clock.

22. In the First World War there were many names for a German. One was 'Bosche' which was the French word for 'rascal'. Others included 'Fritz', 'Jerry' and 'Johnny'.

23. Physical Training Instructor.

24. North Somerset Yeomanry.

25. In the First World War the Germans used dogs to carry messages.

26. Northumberland Fusiliers.

27. Field Ambulances were not ambulances as we know them today. They comprised a couple of hundred non-combatant men and were attached to a Brigade, moving with them as necessary. They provided one or more Advanced Dressing Stations in reasonable proximity of the front line and casualties would be transferred from here to the Clearing Stations.

28. According to the records of the 25th Division, a Lieutenant E. W. Pickles of the 3rd Worcesters was awarded a Military Cross because: 'On 27th May, 1918, at Concevreux this officer displayed great gallantry and devotion to duty. His battalion was retiring and closely followed by the enemy, and it seemed just possible that heavy casualties would be inflicted before another position could be taken up. Grasping the situation, 2nd Lieutenant Pickles collected some 20 men, turned and attacked the enemy with such effect that the whole advance in that neighbourhood was checked for at least an hour.' Perhaps this was the 'regrouping' to which my father refers.

29. Red Cross.

30. Battery Sergeant Major of Royal Field Artillery.

31. High Explosives.